REASONS FOR FAITH

REASONS
FOR
FAITH

John H. Gerstner

Soli Deo Gloria Publications
...for instruction in righteousness...

Soli Deo Gloria Publications
A division of Soli Deo Gloria Ministries, Inc.
P.O. Box 451, Morgan, PA 15064
(412) 221-1901/FAX 221-1902
www.SDGbooks.com

*

Reasons for Faith was first published by Harper & Brothers
Publishers, New York. This Soli Deo Gloria reprint is 1995.
Printed in the USA. All rights reserved.

*

ISBN 1-57358-021-X
Library of Congress Catalog Card Number 60-5294

*

Third Printing 2004

To Dr. John Orr:
Teacher, counselor, friend

Contents

IV. A CONSIDERATION OF SOME OBJECTIONS TO CHRISTIANITY

V. CONCLUSION

Preface

THIS book has been written because a friend, whose suggestions have always carried the force of commands with me, a long time ago urged me to write it. He knows this field far better than I, and since he said that there was a need for such a work, I assumed it was true.

It did not follow that I was the one to attempt to meet this need. My friend, for one, was far better qualified than I, as I told him more than once. But since his suggestions are my commands, not mine his, I wrote the book. I laid down one stipulation, however: that he read and criticize the manuscript. This he has done, for which I am most grateful. He has also done me another and still greater favor in permitting me to dedicate the book to him. He disavows that he deserves the honor, but since I think it is the book, not he, that is honored, the matter stands.

There were others who have encouraged me, helped me by criticisms, and by their over-all contribution kept the volume from being even more unworthy than it is. I refer to the one who is my helpmate in every thing, my wife—no mean apologist, I may add. Also, I would thank my dear friend Addison H. Leitch for his good offices. Nor would I forget to acknowledge those academic guinea pigs at Campus-in-the-

Woods, Ontario, Canada, August 1958, who very graciously read several chapters to let me know whether I was speaking, non-technically, to mid-twentieth-century collegians. They thought that I was. I hope that they were right, for though this book is meant for everyone in general, it is meant for college students in particular.

One technical note needs to be added. Those learned in philosophy and theology will immediately recognize that this book takes the position of the older, rather than the more recent, Christian apologists. This I do, not because I prefer the old as such, and certainly not because I have not read and wrestled with the new, but simply because I am not persuaded by the less rational approaches of today. I do not much discuss these intramural differences, not because they are not important, but simply because they seem to have no proper place in a volume meant for the general thinking public and not for the specialists.

PART I

INTRODUCTION

1

I Believe

WE BEGIN our discussion with the observation that many
today are disposed to belief. What the nature and value of
this belief may be we do not at first attempt to estimate. It
is enough to observe that this is, in a sense, a believing world
and a believing century. At the same time, there are some
very formidable forces tending toward unbelief. These we
examine in the second chapter. Following this we come to
the argument proper of the book.

We must always begin where we are. So we begin with ourselves as we find ourselves and show the significance of our
situation for an approach to the question of Christianity. In
the third chapter we show that we are thinking souls, capable
of faith when proper evidence is presented. Then, looking at
the world round about us, we seek to learn what it tells, if
anything, of God and our relation to Him (chapters 4 and
5). We find evidence in nature for the existence of God as
an ultimate cause and a personal, eternal, moral spirit. But
in the sixth chapter we consider some of the arguments
against these theistic conclusions.

The third part of the volume deals with the truth of Christianity, and first of all, in the seventh chapter, we note what nature reveals about God and what it leaves unsaid. The eighth chapter attempts to show that the Bible answers the important questions which nature leaves unresolved, while the ninth chapter presents the argument for the Bible as revelation. The next two chapters consider some of the miracles of the Bible and their cogency as an argument for its supernatural character. The twelfth chapter does the same with the prophecies of the Bible. The bearing of archaeology on the authenticity of the Bible is next weighed (13). In the following chapters we try to present the broad outline of the Christian religion as it is set forth in the Bible (14), consider some of the difficulties in this religion (15), and compare it in its salient features with the major religions of the world (16). The last four chapters of this section all deal with the influence of Christianity. The first two (17, 18) survey its broad social contribution, while the other two are narrower in scope, the nineteenth chapter presenting the argument from one's personal experience of Christ and the last, from the experience and witness of the martyrs.

The fourth part of the book takes up a consideration of objections to Christianity from evolution (21), determinism (22), Biblical criticism (23), and the shortcomings of the church (24). We conclude with the "pragmatic test."

This, then, is a brief sketch of what I hope to prove. How successful my attempt is, I must leave the reader to judge. But now let us begin by noticing the belief of our day. Dr. H. S. Coffin is said to have begun a sermon with the Psalmist's question: "If the foundations be destroyed what can the righteous do?" To which he immediately answered: "Why, go on being righteous, of course!" We are not so sure of the rightness of that reply, but it is clear that although the traditional foundations of religious faith have been badly damaged in the minds of many, they have gone on believing.

There are at least eight different and significant indications that this is a believing world. First, the recent wars revealed widespread faith. Second, the present world crisis has precipitated a universal affirmation of faith. Third, there are numerous popular demonstrations of faith. Fourth, the great increase in church membership is an indication of faith. Fifth, the conservative drift in Biblical Criticism is another telltale sign. Sixth, widespread religious education movements are based on and appeal to faith. Seventh, many intellectuals are shouting their credos from the housetops. Eighth, the development of irrationalism in all fields of science and art is meant to provide, by denying the sufficiency of reason, a basis for faith.

First, whatever questions may be raised concerning the quality, the motivation, or the permanence of "foxhole religion," there can be no doubt that the recent wars did reveal a widespread faith. Men in battle, fliers on solitary vigil, prisoners of war, and lonely homesick men testify to an experience of God. Soldiers from the South Pacific to North India saw the humane effects of Christian missions and bore it witness—the khaki viewpoint. Even the popular military songs—not to mention others—were religious in theme: "God Bless America," "Coming in on a Wing and a Prayer," "Praise the Lord and Pass the Ammunition." We do not contend that all of this faith was of the most devout sort, but the point is that it was indicative of a conviction that there is a God who can be known and felt.

Second, even more than the war, the postwar crisis has precipitated a latent faith. Men of science, educators, statesmen, military leaders, no less than churchmen, have declared that the only hope of the hour is religious conviction. Alarmed by the fact that man can communicate with the moon and outer space but not with his fellow man across a conference table, the world has become desperate. Finding that they can fly in the air like a bird and go over the water and under it like a fish, but that he cannot walk on the earth with his fellow man, many have become extremely distressed. In this desperation the world has come to second the Church's motion that man must know God before he can know himself or his neighbor. The vertical relation must precede the horizontal. Religion is more fundamental than morals. The need, as General Douglas MacArthur once stated, is "theological." In severing morals from religion we have lost both. Ours is a "cut-flower" civilzation with the theological root severed and the flower fading.

Third, numerous popular phenomena are indicative of a basic religious conviction on the part of the rank and file. In Russia, Communism has had to yield ground to the irrepressible religious belief of the people. Germany has seen a resurgence of Biblical Christianity. England not so long ago was showing as much enthusiasm for C. S. Lewis' religious broadcasts as America used to show for Amos and Andy. Dorothy Sayers, of detective fiction fame, also wrote of religion, and the masses read it. In America, some religious books are among the best sellers, and evangelistic preaching is bringing the greatest religious crowds known to history. Newspapers devote considerable attention to religious opinion, and syndicated articles are more and more in evidence. Entrance of laymen into church activity and leadership and the increasing number of women trained for religious vocations spell broadening public interest in the Church and its cause.

Fourth, greatly increased church membership, especially in the United States, is another straw in the wind. It must be remembered that only certain churches, i.e., the Roman Catholic, count baptized children. The millions of Baptists are all adults. Figures are lacking on those churches which in principle include baptized children as noncommunicant members but in practice do not always count them. It would be safe to say that the number of members, if all baptized children were listed, would exceed the official figures by five million. This membership is both an absolute and a relative growth. That is, there are not only many more church members today than in 1890 but the percentage is also much higher. In 1890, 20 per cent of the population were on the church rolls; in 1944, 52 per cent were.

Fifth, in scholarly circles there is a notable drift toward a conservative view of the Bible. The tendency prevails in theology, but we are now thinking of the conservative drift in textual criticism. The nineteenth century wrought havoc with the traditional view of the Bible and attempted to undermine its fundamental authenticity as a historical document. Increasingly in the twentieth century these "assured results of criticism" have become less and less assured. In the New Testament field, for instance, Paul's epistles have been almost completely recognized as authentic. The Gospel of John is now acknowledged to be a first-century document. Jesus, as a historical character, is no longer questioned; His supernatural person and acts are admittedly a part of the record. Overwhelming evidence of manuscripts and versions attests to the genuineness of the New Testament story.

If anything, Old Testament criticism reflects the drift even more clearly. No less an archaeologist-linguist-critic than W. F. Albright contends powerfully for the monotheism of Moses; Heidel shows the significant differences between the Old Testament and the Babylonian Creation and Flood stories and indicates a unique, determinative set of beliefs in ancient Israel; Thiele demonstrates the historical accuracy of Kings; Allis restates the case for Mosaic authorship and is often ridiculed but never refuted. The general trend is to find unity rather than a destructive disunity in the Bible.

And what Meek affirmed in 1946 is more true today (as the

Twentieth Century Encyclopedia of Religious Knowledge [ed., L. A. Loetscher] reveals in many of its articles):

There is no question that Old Testament scholarship is definitely more conservative. This is partly due to the natural reaction against the extremes of the preceding age; it is partly due to the current interest in archaeology, which is supposed to confirm much in the Bible; and it is partly due to the influence of Barthian theology. The trend is apparent in Germany where the school of Albrecht Alt dominates the Old Testament field; it is apparent in the numerous publications of the Hebrew University in Jerusalem; it is apparent in Sweden in the school of Johannes Pedersen; it is apparent in the writings of H. H. Rowley, one of the most prolific of British Old Testament scholars; and it is apparent in the work of America's most distinguished scholar, W. F. Albright. Indeed, the latter goes so far as to affirm that the Hebrew religion did not change in fundamentals from the time of Moses until the time of Christ.

Sixth, widespread religious education movements reveal the inclination toward faith. Sorokin, in his *Crisis of Our Age*, shows the almost 100 per cent religious character of the education and culture in the twelfth century in comparison with the almost 100 per cent secularism of the twentieth. By way of reaction, the past few decades have unleashed a great number of Character Education Courses, released-time religious education courses, and the like. Psychology has stressed the need of motivation for noble democratic living, and religion is increasingly being called on to provide it. The lack of someone who can make virtue more attractive than vice has made education a tutor to bring men to Christ. While the religious education movement involves some problems concerning the relation of church and state, the fact that the movement is forging ahead steadily indicates the more clearly its power.

Seventh, a notable galaxy of scholars has clustered in the

religious firmament. At the same time that Adler has been agitating that the professor is public enemy number one as an underminer of religion, many learned men have been delivering manifestoes of faith. Their statements are seldom theologically precise, but in a general way they have testified of their genuine religious ardor. Einstein not only bore witness to the heroism of the Christian Church in prewar Germany but made room for God in his thinking. Milliken, Jeans, Eddington, Compton, Hutchins, Whitehead, Hocking, DuNoüy, Franck, Haldane, and Smuts are but a selective list of learned contemporary believers in an eternal being.

The eighth and final evidence of the developing faith of our day is, strangely enough, "irrationalism. That there has been a revolt against reason no one can ignore. Freudian psychologists have tended to reduce rational thought to rationalization, making the nonrational *libido* or *id* the father of thought. Cubism, surrealism, and abstractionism have been so many artistic attempts to get beneath outer reason. Dostoievski, Mann, Joyce, and others have been concerned with something they believe to be profounder than the thinking of their literary creatures. "Scotfree verse," "Steinese," et cetera, show poetry to be accessible. Progressive Education's emphasis on "attitude" more than, if not rather than, on "content" is another case in point. In a basic sense, Kant began the philosophic revolt against reason, but the insurrection has reached a much more advanced stage in the existentialism of Jaspers and Heidegger and the mysticism of Unamuno. It was Kierkegaard who, in theology, tried to say the irrational is the real; while Barth, in spite of his opposition to system, has tried to systematize this theological irrationalism. In Brunner, Reinhold Niebuhr, and Tillich one sees emerging from the revolutionists themselves the beginning of a revolt against the revolt against reason.

We cite this attempt to get "beyond the beyond," as

Stephen Leacock describes it, merely because we interpret it as a desperate attempt to provide in irrationalism a basis for belief. These thinkers seem to feel, as so many ordinary people do, that reason is an obstacle to faith. It must therefore be gotten out of the way. We do not believe that can be done, but the point we are noting here is that the very attempt of these scholars to do the impossible reveals the desperate desire of the heart to believe. William James' *Will to Believe* had been better entitled the *Right to Believe*, because in it he tried to show that there is no compelling reason why a person may not believe if he wants to. And so say our irrationalists. Their method may be hopeless but the aim is significant. It reminds one of Jesus' words to the disciples when they hailed His Triumphal Entry: "I tell you, if these were silent, the very stones would cry out" (Luke 19:40). Here are the philosophical stones of irrationalism crying out their Hosannas. Here are modern Nicodemuses coming to Jesus by metaphysical night.

Studdert-Kennedy has expressed this irrepressible desire to believe even when one thinks the intellectual obstacles are insurmountable:

How do I know that God is good? I don't. I gamble like a man. I bet my life upon one side in life's great war. I must, I can't stand out. I must take sides. The man who is neutral in this fight is not a man. He's bulk and body without breath, cold leg of lamb without mint sauce. A fool. He makes me sick. Good Lord! Weak tea! Cold slops! I want to live, live out, not wobble through my life somehow, and then into the dark. I must have God. This life's too dull without, too dull for aught but suicide. What's a man to live for else? I'd murder some one just to see red blood. I'd drink myself blind drunk, and see blue snakes if I could not look up to see blue skies, and hear God speaking through the silence of the stars. How is it proved? It isn't proved, you fool, it can't be proved.

. . . . .

I am no fool, I have my reasons for this faith, but they are not the reasonings, the coldly calculated formulae of thought divorced from feeling. They are true, too true for that.

We think this is nonsense—madness. But it is a sublime madness, and insane sanity. Men must have God and it seems they will have Him by mental hook or crook. The following pages are meant to present a rational approach to our deepest and most irrepressible need—God.

2

Help Thou Mine Unbelief

ALONGSIDE of the factors that make for faith, indicated in the last chapter, there are those which tend to undermine religious certitude. In this chapter we will consider the big three: secularism, scientism, and suffering. Some one or a combination of these will likely be seen to be the cause of that unbelief.

Secularism in simpler language is merely worldliness; or "this-worldliness" in contrast to "other-worldliness." This one-world-at-a-time philosophy sees the future as an irrelevance, if not an impertinence. It supposes that one world in the hand is worth two in the bush. What does it profit a man if he saves his soul but loses the whole world? It allows religion only if it is practical, i.e., useful in this world. And the true God can be accepted only if He will help in the service of the god which is the world.

We may notice that area where, until recently, secularism was most seriously evident—the public schools. The United States has devolved from a religiously oriented philosophy of education to one from which religion has been almost completely excluded. Freedom of religion has relentlessly developed into freedom from religion. The reaction is now upon us with weekday, released-time religious education sweeping the nation and parochial schools more and more vigorously expanding and demanding state support. But along all the fronts, sacred and secular, the cry is the same: "Down with Secularism—in Education."

We do not infer that all of the trend toward secularism is wrong nor that all of the medieval and early Protestant emphasis was right. As a matter of fact, it was some of the extremes of medieval society which necessitated the modern reaction. Howbeit, modernism has gone to another and far worse extreme. The Renaissance, which in a sense was the spearhead of the modern secular invasion, had within itself the seeds of wholesome correction and extreme reaction. In the art of that period, for example, we find introduced a healthy realism, an interest in landscape, perspective, foreshortening, and a careful delineation of human emotion and physique. All of these marked valuable discoveries or recoveries that immensely enriched the staid, idealized, unreal tendencies in the art of the Middle Ages. Nevertheless, the other seed of the Renaissance was secularism or the worship of this world, and that unfortunately is a great obstacle to true worship.

The trouble with secularism is the world itself. It always proves to be a mere shadow. Those who are most successful in acquiring it suffer the greatest disillusionment. It is a notorious fact that the wealthiest persons, unless they be truly religious persons, are the most bored, the least happy. They are always piling up but never possessing anything. Their experiences, like the Preacher's, lead to the dirge: "All is vanity and vexation of spirit under the sun." Secularists are bent on pleasure, but "she that liveth in pleasure is dead while she liveth." Animals can eat, drink, and be contented, but man cannot. He cannot be contented without these physical gratifications because he has his animal appetites, but being more than an animal he cannot be content with only them. He cannot live without bread, but neither can he live by bread alone.

The second cardinal defect in secularism is the loss of the other world which it spurns. Man cannot be happy with this world, nor can he be happy without the other. Even if he disbelieves the other world he cannot escape it. He cannot escape it even now. He cannot be sure that there is not an eternal world. He may disbelieve it, but he cannot, try as he will, disprove it. As Shakespeare has said, he is afraid to "shuffle off this mortal coil" with all its griefs because he does not know what lies ahead. He may have doubts about God, but who has ever demonstrated His nonexistence? How can man satisfy himself that there is no heaven which he may miss nor any hell which he may enter? The slightest possibility of these things—and who can deny their possibility?—utterly unnerves the secularist.

If there were any satisfaction in the possession of the whole world for a lifetime, how would that compensate for one moment out of heaven or one moment in hell? The merest possibility of the eternal world completely outweighs the utmost certainty of this one. What answer, therefore, can a worldling give to Jesus' question, "What does it profit a man if he gain the whole world and lose his own soul?" It will not comfort him to reply, "But I do not believe you. I do not believe that I, in gaining the whole world, will forfeit my own soul." It will not comfort him because he is not sure that he is right, nor certain that Christ is wrong. The mere possibility that Christ's question about the future is valid ruins his present. "To him that hath not shall be taken away even that which he hath"—from him that has not the world to come shall be taken away even this one which he has.

Scientism is an intellectual disease which cuts its victim

off from everything in the world which is not known by the senses. The inevitable symptom of this is "negativitis." The victim will find it necessary to deny everything of an ideal character. "Is there a God?" "Put Him in a beaker and I will believe." "Are there spiritual values?" "Seeing is believing." "Is love real?" "Test it with litmus paper." "What is justice?" "Give me a sample and I'll see how it reacts with sulphuric acid." If anything does not conform to these criteria of sense, it simply does not exist. It is an illusion, a fantasy, a superstition.

Scientism is inimical to faith because it makes it either superfluous or illusory. Let a man breathe this atmosphere long enough to contract the infection and he will, as many have done, come to the unscientific conclusion that science is all there is, and scientific methodology, so admirably adapted to scientific knowledge, is the open-sesame to all knowledge.

Mostly nonscientists suffer from scientism simply because, not knowing the true spirit of science, they make unfounded generalizations. Einstein constantly emphasized the vast unknown, but the man on the street is confident that science is the key to omniscience. Eddington and Jeans have found too much mystery in the universe to deny God, but those of little learning cannot admit into their thinking anyone bigger than their own minds. Edison said that no man knew one seven-billioneth of 1 per cent ($\frac{1}{7,000,000,000}$ x 1%) about anything, but the man who reads by Edison's light bulbs finds the universe an open book.

True science is suckled at the breast of faith, takes its first step holding the hand of faith, walks by faith, and arrives at a goal of faith. Before a man can think he must exercise faith in his reason. He cannot examine a test tube without relying on his eyes. Nor can he draw a conclusion without positing the reliability of the laws of inference. He deals with effects such as movement, heat, and color, all of which are, according to scientific inference, caused by *invisible* particles or units of energy which are believed to be there. And the final conclusion toward which science ever tends is a confidence in the uniformity of nature which is merely a strong supposition that because what was observed in the past has behaved according to a certain pattern, it will continue to do so in the future.

It is interesting that the most exact of all the sciences, mathematics, is most clearly based on faith. Have you ever seen a mathematical dot, which is a point without dimension? Have you ever seen a mathematical line, which is length without thickness? Have you ever seen a mathematical square, which possesses length and width but no depth? To be sure, we may conceive what we cannot visualize, but so soon as that distinction is recognized, we are inoculated against scientism.

Is it not remarkable that Jesus' explanation of the working of the Holy Spirit in the human heart is rather analogous to the scientists' explanation of the operation of atomic energy? Christ said, "The wind bloweth where it listeth, and thou hearest the sound thereof, but canst not tell whence it cometh, and whither it goeth: so is every one that is born of the Spirit" (John 3:8). That is, we cannot see the windlike Holy Spirit, but His presence is indicated by His effects which are clearly visible in the hearts of men. Similarly, our scientists say that atomic energy is invisible, but its presence is evident in the powerful effects which it produces.

Many years ago Henry Drummond spoke of the *Natural Law in the Spiritual World.* He reminded us that science tends toward faith and not away from it provided we avoid scientism, which denies too much because it knows too little.

That which troubles the belief of people most is just trouble. How often do we hear people say, "I believed in God until my child was struck by an automobile." "If there be a God how can He permit this war?" "If God is in His Heaven how can there be such misery on His earth?"

Nor does suffering disturb the faith of the simpler-minded only. Philosophers are even more distressed by it. Those who think most deeply feel this problem most keenly, and every philosophy must face it and render an explanation. How impatient was William James with philosophies which merely thought things good rather than tried to make them so. Nor would he allow the problem of evil to be dissolved by reducing its dimensions. In his characteristically lively way he said that we have the problem of evil so long as one cockroach suffers from unrequited love.

The unbelief occasioned by the problem of evil may express itself in several ways. For one thing, a person may be led to deny some of God's attributes. That is to say, he may deny God's attributes without denying His existence. Thus he may question God's goodness, saying that God, rather than being opposed to evil, is indifferent to it. He is "beyond good and evil": both are the same to Him. With ruthless indiscrimination He decrees whatever comes to pass. This fatalistic conception has been taken up into some non-Christian theologies. It has been expressed by the nontheological Ed Wynn thus:

> There is a divinity that shapes our ends rough,
> Hew them how we may.

However religiously this fatalism may be expressed it is still unbelief—certainly in the goodness if not the being of God.

If this first form of unbelief sacrifices God's goodness to His power, the second form sacrifices His power to His goodness. On the one hand, it is said God is certainly powerful, and since He does not prevent evil, He must not be altogether good. Or, on the other hand, it is said that God is certainly good, and since He does not prevent evil, He must not be altogether powerful. He wants to eliminate evil, and He is partly successful in overcoming it but not completely. Plato found a recalcitrant element outside of God which prevented the full expression of the Highest Idea or the Good. Brightman internalized this element which he called the "Given" and saw a "finite God" struggling with himself. But whether a dualist like Plato, a mystic like Böhme, a pragmatist like James, or limited theists like Brightman and Berdyaev, they all solve the problem of evil by yielding belief in God—or in some of the attributes of God.

While it is not our purpose here to deal exhaustively with this greatest of all problems, we do mention a few factors which relieve some of the intellectual tension. First, we are nearsighted creatures. Our finitude robs us of the full view. Bad perspective creates a foreshortening. That is to say, good often appears to be evil, because of our narrow vision. Obstacle courses which seemed burdensome evils at the time may later turn out to have been unmitigated goods.

Second, suffering is frequently productive of good and not evil. It is proverbial that great artists, especially musicians, have been great sufferers. Some have gone to the extreme of saying that evil is necessary for the development of good.

Third, suffering occasions good to others. As Jesus said of the man born blind: "Neither hath this man sinned, nor his parents; but that the works of God should be made manifest in him" (John 9:3).

Fourth, many feel that the ultimate argument is that the freedom of man necessarily entails the possibility of his doing evil and bringing suffering upon himself and others. We do not concede this, but we do make capital of the recognition that some evil stems from human freedom, and we underline man's consciousness of guilt and responsibility. We go so far as to say that the sin and guilt of man are such that his problem is really not one of suffering, which may be the deserved punishment for evil-doing, but is rather one of undeserved good. In other words, we have a problem not of adversity but of prosperity. Indeed Christ reflects on this problem of good when He says that God makes His "sun to shine on the unjust." The very fact that men rarely reflect on the undeserved favor of God, rather implies that we deserve the punishment (suffering) of which we complain.

While we do not believe that personal freedom is the ultimate explanation of the origin of evil, we do believe that freedom was the means by which sin did come into the world. And while what we are about to say is anticipating some things which have not as yet been proved, it may be wise to say them at this point because the problem of evil is such a pressing one for us all.

Christianity teaches that the wages of sin is death (Rom. 6:23). It is not natural for man to die; death is the consequence of evil-doing. Whatever a man sows that shall he reap is the teaching of the Bible (Gal. 6:7). When man was first made by the Creator, he was born into an ideal world without pain or suffering or death (Gen. 1-3). When he is ultimately redeemed and glorified, he will live in a world where there shall be no tears forevermore (Rev. 7:17). In other words, sin and suffering are functions of each other. One does not occur without the other. At the same time, the Bible warns us against thinking that suffering in this world is proportionate to the evil done (Luke 13:1 ff.). On the contrary, this world is a period of probation, and the real judgment for good or evil takes place at death. So while we may say that were there no sin there would be no suffering, we cannot say that one man suffers more than another because he is a greater sinner than the other.

Christianity further teaches that sin is committed against God and is therefore an infinitely heinous crime deserving the most awful judgment (Ps. 51). In comparison with what sinners actually deserve, their most severe sufferings in this world are not punishments but mere warnings of the wrath which is to come. "Vengeance is mine; I will repay, saith the Lord" (Rom. 12:19).

If these things be so (and we are not here attempting to prove them) a very great light falls on the problem of human suffering. Indeed, its whole character changes. The worst suffering which any man is ever called upon to endure in this world is basically merciful in character! It is in no sense proportionate to what the best man deserves. Mind you, we are not now claiming that the Christian view of sin, guilt, and suffering is true. We ask the reader to suspend his judgment on this matter for the moment, remembering only that the religion which he is about to consider, if it *be* true, answers the greatest problem which has ever agitated the mind and heart of suffering mankind.

To summarize. Much that we call evil only appears to be so because our finite judgment lacks perspective. But even real evil may frequently, perhaps always, be of benefit to ourselves and others. If, however, there be a kind of evil which is absolutely and irreducibly evil, it is traceable to man, not to God. And the only mystery about evil is why God tolerates it—a "mystery," mark you (something known but incapable of being perfectly understood) rather than a "problem" (something incapable of being understood even partially).

PART II

ON THE EXISTENCE OF GOD

3

The Starting Point

THE first thing of which we human beings are conscious
is probably not ourselves, but the world about us. As soon as
we are born we become conscious of ourselves in relation to
an environment, however inarticulate in infancy that consciousness may be. We are experiencing this world; we are
other than this world. And it is over against this not-self
that we recognize the self.

So we ask where we should begin our argument—with the
world with which we actually begin our thinking and consciousness, or with ourselves who begin there? We think it
best to follow the logical rather than the chronological order
and consider first ourselves, the experiencing agents, before
we consider what we experience. Why? Simply because the
validity of our experiencing must depend on the experiencer;
namely, on ourselves. So let us begin with ourselves. Although
that is not the natural order, it seems the best order for
thinking.

Beginning with ourselves what do we find? We find bodies,
in union with which there is a "something other," which
reflects on this body and thinks about it and evaluates the data

which come to it through the senses of the body. Whatever this "other" is, it is other. It is not body, for it thinks of body as objective and different from itself. If this is an illusion, there is no way of knowing it, for the "other" is the only means by which we know anything. If the "other" is not other, there is nothing besides it which could reveal that fact. So we must assume that the "other" is other, because it indicates that it is other and it is the only source of information that we have.

But the fact that this "other" is other does not mean necessarily that it is of a different nature from the body of which it is aware. Conceivably it could be a different body, invisible and smaller perhaps, maybe within the outer body. Let us consider that. The outer body is visible, but the "other" is not visible; the outer body is tangible, but the "other" is not tangible; the outer body is measurable, but the "other" is not measurable. So far we can know that our body deals directly with tangibles and measurables, but the "other" deals with them differently. So far as we know it does not come into contact with them, it does not hold them as on a scale, it does not see them with any eyes such as those of the body. It deals with these tangibles as abstractions; we shall call them for want of a better word, ideas. These ideas don't weigh anything, have no odor, are not visible. Therefore, the "other" that deals with such things must be quite different from the body—quite different indeed. And it can do things with ideas that the body cannot do with its objects. The body can only feel the object when it is present, but the "other" can deal with ideas when no-thing is present. Again, the body can sense some things as combined only if they are combined, and, unless they are in some manner combined, it does not see them that way. But the "other" can combine ideas at will and recombine them and arrange them differently from their first order. And, indeed, as we get better acquainted with the "other," we find that it can deal with ideas that apparently never came through the body at all.

Everything considered, this "other" must be not only numerically but qualitatively different. So let us give it a different and more distinguishing name; let us call it spirit, mind, or soul. So far we know very little about this soul, but we do know one all-important thing: it is the means by which we know what we know and learn what we learn. From this viewpoint it is all-important. Without it we cannot know anything; we simply cannot find any other thing in our make-up by which we can learn a thing. We are utterly dependent on this soul of ours even for a knowledge of the soul.

We simply have to trust the soul. We are in the same relation to it that the disciples of Jesus were to Him. When others left Jesus and He asked them if they too would leave, they replied, "But to whom else can we go?" If we should leave this soul of ours as a source of information, to what else could we go? There is no other means given to men whereby they may know anything. If they cannot know by this means they cannot know by any means, for there are no others.

We cannot doubt the soul. In the very act of doubting we must assume that we are, even while we doubt that we are. It is we who doubt that we are! That is the same as to say again, we have no other means of thinking at all than this. If we think that we cannot trust our thinking, we must trust our thinking that we cannot trust our thinking. If we doubt, we must trust the minds which doubt, and thus we must not doubt if we would doubt. There just is no escape from dependence on the mind; for if we would escape, we must rely on the mind in the very "woulding." So if we would, we would not after all. For the mind to get out of the mind is as for the body to get out of its skin. If the body got out of its skin, it would not be the body any more; if the mind got out of the mind, it would not be the mind any more. We simply must begin here—not only because there is no place else to begin, but because if we think that we will not begin here, it is here that we are thinking that we will not begin.

This matter is so important that we must go into a more thorough discussion of skepticism. If credulity was common in the medieval era and superstition in primitive culture, the problem of knowledge from which many moderns suffer is skepticism. Proceeding from the true statement that it is the mark of a scholar at times to suspend judgment, many have jumped to the conclusion that the certain way to intellectual glory is to be uncertain about everything. Many modern scholars have no definite opinions on anything except the definite opinion that one should never have a definite opinion. They seem to live in mortal fear of coming to a conclusion—"ever learning and never coming to the knowledge of the truth." As a dog will chase a cat until he is about to catch it and then turn tail and run, so they love the pursuit of wisdom so long as they are sure that they can never catch up to it. "I disbelieve," they say; "help thou my belief." And this attitude they describe as "detached," "impartial," "objective."

Skepticism produces two diagonally opposed outlooks, as we shall see. First, the skeptic maintains, no one can know anything (except, of course, the skeptic, who knows this much). And then he finds himself concluding that since no one knows anything, everyone's knowledge is as good as everyone else's. So very tolerantly he says your knowledge is true for you and my knowledge is true for me precisely because no one knows anything anyway. It therefore comes to pass that because no one knows anything, everyone knows everything.

Going into a bit more detail, we examine first this skeptical notion (and we hope that the reader does not fail to notice that the skeptic is never skeptical of his skeptical notions) that no one knows anything. The theory is self-contradictory. It professes to be skeptical about everything, but, as a matter of fact, it is not at all skeptical of its own skepticism. It has no doubt that every thing is doubtful. This position is manifestly untenable. For if we accept the skeptical conclusion, we have to be unskeptical to do so. Or if we are skeptical even about skepticism, we cannot be skeptical. In other words, to be skeptical a person must not be skeptical. A theoretical house divided against itself simply cannot stand.

But in the second place, skepticism is false, not only because it is internally contradictory, but also because it rests on a false theory of knowledge. It suspects all propositions because they are made by finite men. It supposes that because men are finite, they will necessarily distort truth by their own prejudices. "That's your interpretation," skeptics will say, as if that observation demonstrates its falsity. But why is it necessarily an untrue interpretation, simply because it is yours? We can see that it may be untrue but why *must* it be so? We can see that a student who has been flunked in an examination might be tempted to think his paper deserved more because he would be prejudiced in his own favor. But there are students who sometimes admit that their exams did not deserve to pass. One cannot assume, even in the case of an interested person, that he will always and necessarily distort objective facts to his own advantage. It is at least possible for a person to consider something detachedly—even for an interested person. And when the element of obvious personal interest is removed, as it is in many judgments, an individual would be inclined to be objective.

In any case, no skeptic could possibly disprove the objectivity of personal interpretations. He must assume objectivity to deny it. He must assume that his judgment is objective to say that yours is not. If he proves that all personal interpretation is subjective and unreliable, he condemns his own judgment including the very judgment that all personal judgment is unreliable.

Third, skepticism is a confusion of a part with the whole. It is true that some judgments are unsound. Therefore, it is wholesome to be "skeptical" or, better, "critical" of all judgments, our own included, until verified. We should examine judgments carefully and impartially. This is the true and wholesome element in skepticism. But the thoroughgoing skeptic confuses the part with the whole. That is, he insists that because some judgments may be proved "subjective," all are necessarily so. He throws out the baby with the bath. It would be better to throw out the bath but keep the baby.

Very well, we are weary of skepticism—weary of trying to escape our minds by our minds. It is a foolish business indeed, and we considered it only for the purpose of showing the futility of it.

So we must begin here, for there is no place else to begin. But suppose someone says, "I will not begin at all; I will not think at all; I will eat, drink, and be merry and never be bothered with Christian evidences"? To such a person we must say, "If you are going to use your mind only for help in eating, drinking, and being merry, it is possible that you may some day be held responsible. It is possible that if you listen to what your mind is saying to you, you would hear it saying, 'You must not eat, drink, and be merry merely. I have higher duties and responsibilities for you. And if you are disobedient, you will some day be severely punished.'" If the person replies, "But I don't know anything about any such duty or responsibility or possible punishment," his mind may justifiably say, "Of course you don't know because you will not listen. You will be punished precisely because you do not know." Some may be inclined to shrug all this off, but they cannot do it with an easy mind. Unless they listen to the dictates of this mind or soul of theirs, they cannot very well know what it will say to them. However man got here, whoever or whatever put him here, it is true, as Aristotle says, that he is a "thinking animal" and think he must. If by honest thinking he may properly conclude that life is eating, drinking, and being merry then let him eat, drink, and be merry. But it is rather difficult to eat, drink, and be merry when one does not know whether that is what he is here to do. We shall suggest throughout this book that the soul or mind will and does show man that he is not here to eat, drink, and be merry in the usual sense of the term.

Very well, we must think. And we dare not think that we need not think. So let us think. We have the instrument (the soul) and we have a body of material (the world around us and the soul itself within us) on which the instrument may operate.

And the first thing we may ask about the world around us is, Why? That is, Why is it here? How is it here? Why is there something rather than nothing?

4

The Theistic Argument (1)

"In the beginning matter created the heaven and the earth." What is the matter with that? Nothing is the matter with that except the matter.

Some years ago A. J. Balfour said, "We know too much about matter to be materialists." There were certain things the matter with matter in those days, there had been before then, there still are, and presumably there always will be. What precisely is the matter with matter?

Matter has a past. That is, the matter with matter is that it had a *mater*. Matter is an effect, produced by an adequate cause. Clearly, that which is itself an effect cannot be the cause of all things. In the beginning matter could not create the heaven and the earth, because matter had first to be created. After matter was made, "the beginning" was no longer. Matter may, in some sense, be a cause, but it also is an effect. That which is an effect cannot itself be the first cause. And only the first cause was in the beginning.

But how do we know that matter is an effect, and not the first cause? If matter were the author of all things, it would be, in the first place, the author of life. But how can it be? Matter itself has no life. It is, by definition, "inanimate." That is Webster speaking. The man on the street has the same idea: "lifeless matter," he calls it.

But, we ask, is matter necessarily lifeless? May it not be animated? Let that possibility be immediately granted. Still, matter is then animated by a vital energy, by an *élan vital*, by an architectonic principle. This life-principle, however, is something distinct from matter—even if thought of as inseparable from it. We say that it animates matter; the principle works through the stuff, there is life in matter. Yet it is not matter that lives, but the spirit in matter. Matter itself cannot account for the life-principle, unless, of course, we wish to posit spontaneous generation. If we did, we would have something without any cause coming out of nothing from which nothing comes. Quite apart from all other objections to this idea, it is sufficient to observe here that it would not aid the case of matter in the slightest. For in the event of spontaneous generation, life would not come out of matter, but out of nothing—which is not the same as matter. Matter is something. So anyway you look at it, matter does not seem able to account for life, even the life within itself, much less outside itself.

But there is more in the universe than mere life. There is intelligent life. There is a kind of life which not only lives but which thinks about living. There is life turning in on itself, studying itself, defining itself, conscious of itself. We are such life ourselves. As we read and think, we are living. While in the stream of life, we are yet spectators of it. Now if matter could not produce plain life (mere animation), how could it produce a thinking being? How could matter, which has no life in itself, actually produce a life which can reflect on matter and tell it that it has no life in itself? The medieval philosophers used to ask, "What is matter?" to which the reply was given, "Never mind." And when they asked, "What is mind?" they would answer, "No matter." Matter is not mind, mind is not matter. They are not father and son, not distantly related, not even in the same family of being.

If matter is tried for the role of creator and found wanting, what of the immaterial? Perhaps force, energy, life, spirit brought all things out of nothing. Let us see. First off, we must say that such a force or energy would have to be self-existent. For if it were not self-existent, it would be dependent on something or someone else and so could not be the ultimate source. It cannot depend on anything but itself if it is to account for everything by itself. So it must be self-existent. And of course if self-existent, it must be eternal. If it were not eternal, then there would have to have been a time when it was not and when something or someone brought it into being. In that case, it could not be the explanation of all things and all persons. So it must be eternal. And it must be personal. For, if it were not personal it must be impersonal. But if it were impersonal how could it have produced persons? How could we ever have come into being to ask questions about something ultimately impersonal which necessarily could not understand our questions, much less answer them? Perhaps, as some like to speculate, the ultimate is *super*personal. Be this as it may, the ultimate can not well be *sub*personal or impersonal and still be the source of a higher kind of being than itself, a being that can ask questions which the ultimate cannot answer.

There is yet another way in which effort has been made to avoid the causal argument. This is the contention that everything came into being by evolution. This view is not associated with anyone in particular because it is more in the nature of a seemingly plausible suggestion than of an actual argument. Most evolutionists, therefore, have not appealed to it. Darwin, for example, believed that God made the original "gemmules" from which the world evolved. Evolution he saw as a subsequent mode rather than an antecedent cause. Most other evolutionists likewise have refrained from suggesting that evolution has anything at all to say about origins.

Nevertheless, some have still professed to believe in "causal evolution." Let us examine the position on the basis of its intrinsic merits. And this is the question we would ask. "If all evolved from evolution, from what did evolution evolve?" If it evolved from something else, we recognize ourselves again in the coils of the infinite regress. And how can there be an evolution that does not evolve? Even if these difficulties were not insuperable, we would face still another dilemma. If evolution were a causal power and if it were self-explanatory, how could it explain anything else? Why is there something (besides evolution) rather than nothing? Evolution, by definition, does not create. But if it cannot create, how can it produce an evolving world? Some would say that it does not *produce* this evolving world, it *is* this evolving world. This, however, is begging the question, for we have already pointed out the difficulty of assuming that the world is just "there." Considerations such as these reveal the wisdom of the vast majority of evolutionists in abstaining from making any causal claims for evolution. We shall have more to say on this subject in a later chapter.

Our world and our universe argue that the cause back of them is one cause. The universe is composed of many parts but one plan. A cosmos, or ordered whole, implies a single ordering mind back of it.

Take but one illustration of the teamwork of the universe, a raindrop. The raindrop falls on the earth and provides the soil with various necessary elements. It is taken up into the trees and flowers and herbs by their various root systems. There the water, by a process called photosynthesis, is transformed into things useful to plant life and released to the air in a gaseous form, ultimately to visit the earth again as a raindrop.

That is a single picture of the unity of our world, the obvious concatenation of its many parts. There is evidence that the universe works as a team. It is a universe and not a "pluriverse." And since we have seen that it must have a cause, the uniformity of it all would suggest the unity of this cause, would it not? Well, not necessarily.

Not necessarily, because it would appear conceivable that there may be many agents working in unison to produce the cosmos. It is a perfectly admissible hypothesis that this universe is the product of many forces or gods working together in perfect unity. How do we find out whether that is so?

First, we have already shown that there can be only one cause behind the universe. Only one independent ultimate cause. That rules out the possibility of there being many. And so while it would be conceivable, so far as the order of the universe alone is considered, that it is the product of many causes working in harmony, this otherwise valid possibility is ruled out by the fact that there can be but one cause. If there should be many causes actually at work producing the unity of the universe, these causes would have to be derivative and therefore but expressions of the purpose of this one cause.

But then, has this "cosmological argument" advanced us? Only in confirming the previous argument. That is, the unity of the world confirms the notion that there is but one cause behind it. In itself it cannot prove that there is, since there could be many harmonious causes working in co-operation. But the world is strictly consistent with the fact that there is but one cause. This argument, therefore, is not independent but corroborative.

There is also much evidence of purpose in this world of ours—at least, things that suggest intelligence. The dandelion sends up a little parachute to carry its seed along on the wind and find a place to germinate. That certainly spells intention. We know from our own experience that we do things like that. We build a house to live in; we make bread to eat. We do things for purposes all the time. William James has defined man as a "fighter for ends." He is a purposive animal. We therefore recognize purpose when we see it. But we search in vain to find anything in the dandelion that corresponds to our brain, the brain that enables us to think up useful plans. And yet the dandelion does things that are every bit as well suited to its purposes as our plans are to ours. Although we cannot find the purpose in the dandelion itself, we do not deny that purpose. We look for it elsewhere. And that "elsewhere" must be the ultimate cause which we have seen lies behind everything that is.

Indeed, when we consider this very purposiveness of ours, we immediately realize that it is not really ours at all. We display it. We are purposive, to be sure. But it is a capacity which was given us. We did not decide to be so. We did not design design. We find ourselves purposive. And while our purposiveness is in ourselves in a sense that the dandelion's purposiveness is not in itself, this is only "in a sense," after all. Our purposive faculty is *in* us, and it is *outside* of the dandelion. But we did not put it in ourselves any more than the dandelion put it outside of itself. There is a purposiveness lying back of both man and dandelion.

And where does it come from? Well we know that it is not in the dandelion itself and that we did not put it in ourselves. It must have come from some other source. We have already shown that the source of all things is the ultimate cause. It must therefore be the cause of purpose as well as everything else. But if it is the author of purpose, it must be purposeful itself; that is, it must be a purposeful cause. Or to put it another way, the first cause must be intelligent.

But the legitimate question arises, "May not the ultimate

cause have been the source of all mere existence, and these mere existences have simply developed, under necessity, their own purposiveness?" Must we conclude that the cause was purposeful because things which originally sprang from it are purposeful? Or to put the question another way, is it not possible that this cause made dandelions and they developed their own method of reproducing themselves? Of course, stating it this way makes the question appear absurd. But do we make it appear any more absurd than it actually is? Do we put the question any other way than the way it must be when we comprehend the nature of the question itself? If this cause did not put a teleological tendency in the things made, must the things made not have developed it themselves? But, if they had to develop it themselves under the exigencies of their situation, they would never have survived the situation in the first place. That is, things need this purposeful activity to survive. Without it in the first place, they could not survive long enough to develop it. Purpose is not the result of the need to survive; survival is the result of purpose.

It is also interesting to consider that for nonpurposive agents to develop purpose, which they did not have to begin with, would be self-contradictory. If they did not have purposive tendencies to begin with why would they develop them? Can you develop intention unintentionally? Can you develop purpose unpurposively? The unpurposing agent would, according to the hypothesis, have unpurposively developed purpose; the unintending agent would unintentionally have developed intention. The opposite must be the case; if the agent was supposed not to have purposiveness, but to have proceeded intentionally to develop it under the exigencies of the situation (in order to survive, for example), the presence of purpose would be proven.

But will someone say that things may have developed purposiveness unpurposefully or accidentally? The very hypothesis, and the only possible hypothesis, rules this possibility out. That is, we are thinking of nonpurposive agents developing purposeful actions that suit them for survival. That is the same as saying that unpurposing agents develop purposive action for the purpose of surviving. The agent is surrounded with a problem, survival. It responds in one way rather than another. Why? Obviously in order to survive. Would some one say it just adapted to its environment without the purpose of surviving? But if it did so adapt itself, we repeat, it must have been a purposeful being at the first.

So then, we know that this ultimate cause is a purposive cause. We know this because everything that comes to pass comes ultimately from this cause, and since purpose or intention come to pass, they must have come ultimately from this cause. And if they came from this cause, this cause must have been purposive for purpose came from it. Could it be possible that purpose came from some other source? It could be—if there were some other source. But we have already shown that there could be no other source. So it must have come from this only possible source. Thus the argument rests on our earlier argument from cause, but it throws further light on the nature of this cause; namely, that it is a purposive cause.

5

The Theistic Argument (2)

ANOTHER thing which we notice in this world of ours is morality or moral consciousness—a sense of right and wrong. Suppose someone attempts to deny this almost universally admitted statement, what then? Well, let us ask him a question. Is our statement that there is a sense of right and wrong, right or wrong? He will reply it is wrong. And if we ask him if his statement that there is no such sense of right and wrong, is right or wrong, he will reply that it is right. So he who denies the sense of right or wrong exercises it himself. Is it right or wrong, reader, to use a sense of right and wrong to deny the existence of a sense of right and wrong?

At this point such a person will protest loudly, saying the above argument is the purest sophistry; that is, it is something that sounds right but is very wrong. So his sense of right and wrong will be further exercised in his denial of the argument for the sense of right and wrong. But overlooking that inconsistency, we will listen as he takes exception to our initial statement that there is such a sense and that his own protest is proof of it. He will say, It is proof of something entirely different; it is proof of a knowledge of right and wrong, not of a sense of right and wrong. It is not proof of a moral sense, but merely of an intellectual judgment, a judgment of "true and false." Now, we will grant that it is proof of a knowledge of right and wrong as intellectually true or false. But if we look more closely, we will see it to be more than that. Granted that we may say of any statement, including the statement that there is a moral sense of right and wrong, that it is right or wrong and mean it in reference to knowledge. Suppose the objector says of our statement (that there is a moral sense of right and wrong) that it is wrong, inasmuch as the supposed "sense" does not exist. Suppose our reply is, "So what? I know that there is no such thing as a moral sense, but I will go on saying there is just the same." Then what? Will our objector let the matter rest? If he wants to be ornery he may; but if he wants to be human, he will say, "It is wrong to say that there is a moral sense of right and wrong when there is none." Now he is not giving a merely intellectual judgment anymore. He is now saying it is wrong as a moral judgment and a matter of feeling. He is not merely coldly intellectual, but warmly moral. Therefore, in any intellectual judgment concerning right and wrong the moral sense is also present. So to make the intellectual statement that there is no sense of right and wrong is self-contradictory because this statement carries with it the moral sense of right and wrong.

What is true in the illustration above is true of all situations. As intellectual beings we judge that certain things are right or wrong. But with that judgment always comes the notion that what we judge to be right, we ought to judge to be right; and what we judge to be wrong, we ought to judge to be wrong. And it would be morally right for us to endorse what is an intellectually right judgment, and it would be morally wrong for us to oppose an intellectually right judgment. As we said, it becomes a matter of feeling, moral feeling. When we see something that we think to be right, we feel under obligation to support it; and when we see something that we think to be wrong, we feel under obligation to oppose it. If we support what we think to be wrong and oppose that which we think to be right, something in us accuses us; but if we support what we think to be right and oppose what we think to be wrong, something in us gratifies us.

This is the basic meaning of the word "conscience." *Conscientia* means "with knowledge." There is something in the human make-up that goes along with knowledge, and this is commonly called conscience. It does not add any information, but it gives color to the information possessed or thought to be possessed. The knowledge may be sound or unsound, well-grounded or ill-grounded, but whatever that knowledge appears to be, this something in man evaluates it in terms of duty. Thus the conscience may be enlightened or it may be unenlightened, depending entirely on the character of the knowledge on which it operates. It in itself, however, is infallible in the sense that it accompanies every judgment. It may be "seared" (that is, one's desires may so incline to a given course of wrong action that they tend to shout down or silence this still small voice of conscience), but the voice is always there and it can always be heard.

What shall we make of this moral consciousness, this conscience of man? Where did it come from? It is in man now, granted. Was it in him at the beginning? Or did he develop it, as he learned to build houses to meet his physical needs? There is a learned symposium entitled *The Dawn of Conscience* (1934), which argues that there was a particular time in human history when conscience first appeared; and those who agree also think that there is a particular time in every individual's life when conscience appears or dawns. We need not pursue any further just how this conscience is thought to dawn. Sufficient for our purposes to note that some think men do develop it themselves to meet their needs as they arise.

So we see that some think that the development of conscience is a purposeful activity on man's part. He develops
conscience because he needs it. We have attempted to show
above that purpose itself must come from an ultimate being.
If, therefore, there is in man a purpose or tendency to develop
a moral nature, it must itself have come from the ultimate
cause. It may, theoretically, have come through man, but it
must have come from the ultimate cause. So on this hypothesis, conscience must be by man but not from man. As he
builds a house, he builds his conscience, maybe. In any case,
the tendency to build a conscience would be from ultimate
cause, just as the tendency to self-preservation would be from
the same source.

But does man really build a conscience as he builds a
house? Does the need for a conscience dawn on man as his
need for shelter dawns on him? Does he some day say, "I ought
to have a sense of 'ought' "?

But there again in the putting of the question we have let
the cat out of the bag. It really isn't possible to develop a
conscience as our hypothesis supposes, because it would represent man as saying, "I ought to have a sense of 'ought.' " Of
course, if he ought to have a sense of "ought," it looks as if
he already has a sense of "ought." His sense of "ought" is
what is actually suggesting to him that he ought to have a
sense of "ought." No one likes to put the question this way,
because it does no credit to his intelligence. So, seeking to
justify himself, a man may say, "What I mean is that men
come to sense a need of an 'ought' faculty. They don't feel
they ought to have a sense of 'ought'; that would be contradictory, admittedly. They just come to think it would be
good or useful to have a sense of 'ought.' They do not feel a
sense of 'ought' in developing a sense of 'ought'; only a sense
of utility." We admit that the statement made that way is not

manifestly contradictory and absurd. But is it true?

Suppose a conscienceless man does say, more or less consciously, "I am going to develop a sense of 'ought' and by this sense judge what things should and should not be done." Is that thinkable? Rather than analyze this in the abstract, let us take a concrete instance. Suppose a person created a sense of the "ought-ness" of doing to others as he would that they should do to him. Applying this self-imposed "ought," he is confronted with this situation: A person who has always hated him, told abominable lies about him, caused him to be demoted, and finally made him lose his job and his reputation, is the only person he knows who has a better knowledge of mathematics than he has. An employer offers him a job with a fabulous salary and great distinction because he thinks him to be the most competent mathematician in a certain territory. The man knows that his enemy is the only better one, but that he *is* better. According to the golden rule, he is under obligation to tell the employer of that fact, because he would want his enemy to do so if the situation were reversed and he were the better of the two mathematicians. The fact that his enemy would not do so, the fact that the last thing in the world he would think of would be the golden rule, is beside the point. The man in question has bound himself by a rule. But the question is, Would the rule hold? Could it be expected to hold? The man would be straining hard. Would the ropes break or not? They would snap like light string. He would not want to be bound, and if he felt for a fleeting moment that he were bound, he would immediately say to himself, "Why should I? I have no obligations except those which I have imposed on myself. Why should I? Why ought I to keep my self-imposed obligation? What obligation have I to keep my obligation?" None at all, of course. He has no obligation to keep self-imposed obligations. If he does feel an obligation to keep self-imposed obligations, the obligation he feels is not itself self-imposed. So the "ought" he has invented has no sense of "ought" at all, unless it is buttressed by a sense of "ought" which he has not invented. Or, to put it the other way, the only hypothesis on which a man's sense of "ought" is binding on him is that which holds that it is not his sense of "ought" at all.

Once again, then, we find that the moral faculty which is in man was not put there by man. Our great and recurring question is, "Whence came this conscience?" And our great and recurring answer is, "It must have come from the first and ultimate cause. Where else?"

So then our first cause is first, ultimate, independent, intelligent and moral in character. "But wait!" someone says. "Why does it follow, because the moral conscience comes from this cause, that the cause itself is moral? Is it not possible that the cause could have produced conscience without possessing it itself? After all, the cause is different from many of the things which have come from it."

Let us suppose that this first cause is itself nonmoral, and that it would say or decree that there should be moral beings in the universe different from itself. This would mean that the cause at least has the idea of conscience in its make-up. It can conceive, at least, of right and wrong and of an agent whose actions are right and wrong. Now, is it possible that it could conceive of such beings and not itself be such a being? If so, it would act without any consciousness of whether it should act or not. It would act intelligently as we have already shown, but it would act without regard to whether the particular action was moral or not. So far as the being is concerned, the action would be action and that is all, not right action. Right action would have no meaning with respect to it. Its creatures could say of their actions that they were right, but that could only mean right with respect to the creature and not with respect to the creator. The creature could pass a judgment on the actions of the creator which even the creator could not pass.

Could there be any incentive for the cause to bring anything else into being if it had no moral consciousness? Granted that it would know how to do so and would have the power to do so. But would it have any incentive to do it if it did not feel that it should do it? Or is this the wrong line of thinking? Anthropomorphic thinking attributing the same kind of functioning to the cause that we are familiar with in men? We must, on the supposition before us, assume that the cause may just do what it does without incentive. It has power and it exerts it; it has intelligence and it uses it. It has no incentive perhaps, but why need it have? Is this conceivable? Is unmotivated power conceivable, power controlled only by intelligence, which would say, "Since you must necessarily function, do it this way"?

Suppose that this power is inertiate, and reason has to say, "You should get a move on and do something." Then power asks, "What?" and reason says, "So and so," and power does it. This would make intelligence determinative of the action of our cause. And so it would have to be, because if power were blind, it would follow that the cause was without intelligence. Since it has intelligence as we have seen, it must evidence it. And therefore it would seem that intelligence would set what wheels are set in motion, in motion. But can reason account for motivation? Reason can say, for example, that power can be exerted in the production of moral agents. Can it do any more than that? Can it somehow say that because power can be so exerted, it shall be? How will it persuade power to act? Merely having a plan along which it can operate would not seem to assure that power will therefore so operate. There could be other plans or there could be inertia. Then what would determine? There seems to be nothing in power or intelligence which provides the necessary motivation that can say to the cause, "Do such and such because you ought to do such and such." It is conceivable that there are beings made by this cause which can operate by mere instinct, but how can an intelligent cause act by mere instinct? That would not be intelligent action. Nor would merely intelligent action really be intelligible or intelligent action. There must be some reason or incentive for using intelligence and power in a particular way. Therefore, it would appear that this cause not only is the source of the "ought," but that it must possess an "ought" itself.

Furthermore, if this cause were not moral, then it would have to be indifferent to moral beings. Although it had made them moral, it would have to be indifferent to whether they function morally or not. They might have a sense that they should do certain things and not do other things, but their author would not care in the slightest what they did. The "ought" in creatures must have a reference outside themselves as we have shown, or else it has no meaning. But to what outside themselves? Hardly to the source from which they came if it is morally disinterested. As a matter of fact, the cause would not even be able to understand what it had produced. If it did understand the sense of "ought," it would have to enforce it. That is, the cause would have to punish the disobedience of conscience. It ought to do that. Not to do so would be a violation of the nature of the creature which the creator had made. And that would be cosmic confusion of the worst sort—unthinkable, unbelievable, immoral, and unintelligent.

But let us go back to the statement, "The cause would have to punish the disobedience of conscience." Not necessarily, someone argues. The cause could have instilled the moral factor in man as an automatic thing. When man obeyed it he would feel good, and when he disobeyed it he would feel bad. The one would be his reward for obedience, and the other his punishment for disobedience. There need not be anything more, leaving the cause itself free to disregard the creature's behavior. But out of this supposition two difficulties arise.

First, if one of the creatures who constantly disregards his moral sense were to avoid the consequences by searing his conscience, what then? That is, if he were to silence his conscience, he would not feel bad, but only indifferent to his violations of it. This would make it possible for him to do evil and not reap any consequence. It would render the moral faculty insignificant and useless. And it would immediately reflect on the intelligence of the cause who, having made a faculty to control men automatically, allowed them to jam it and prevent the thing from working as it was intended. Would not the vast majority of men, if not all, then jam their moral works too, so that they could sin with impunity? Even on our supposition that the cause is not itself moral but is wholly indifferent to morality, it would now be embarrassed as unintelligent. The supreme intelligence would here be outwitted by mere creatures—an inconceivable state of affairs.

But there is a second problem: the prosperity of the wicked. Many of those who stifle their consciences can and indeed do prosper so far as this world is concerned. The racketeer takes what he wants, liquidating any who, in the interests of conscience, oppose him. Now if the intelligent cause were morally indifferent to all this, it would appear that the person who most thoroughly violates the moral faculty with which he is endowed has the universe on his side. The stars in their courses now fight for, rather than against, Sisera. Therefore the cause would be doubly embarrassed: the violator of its moral built-in regulator could not only stifle this regulator but would be rewarded by the outside order of things for so doing.

It would seem, therefore, that if the cause is not moral it

is not intelligent either. If it produces morality in others without possessing it in itself, then it is not wise. As we have attempted to show, the creatures would be able to function better by disregarding their consciences. So if the cause is intelligent, it cannot be nonmoral. Or, positively speaking, if the cause is intelligent it must be moral also.

And so we come to our composite picture—there must be an ultimate cause which is intelligent and moral. The great question now before us is: Is this cause personal? We already have shown it to have various qualities that are essential to personality: power to act, intelligence, and moral consciousness. It would seem that there is but one thing essential to personality that we have not yet found the cause possessing. That is self-consciousness.

Is the cause self-conscious? Is it aware of what it is doing? Does it reflect upon its actions? Does it pass judgments on its thoughts and actions and moral feelings? Well, it either does or it does not. Let us suppose that it does not and therefore lacks an essential part of personality. This would mean that the cause does intelligent acts without an awareness that it does them. Now is that possible? Can anything do an intelligent act without being aware that it is doing it? "Yes," you reply, "take your dandelion as an example. It grows and reproduces in a very intelligent manner, yet there is no evidence that it is conscious of it. May not the cause be like the dandelion which it made?" Hardly, because, as we have earlier shown, the very fact that the dandelion itself does not show signs of deliberate intelligence makes us look elsewhere for the secret of its intelligent actions. There must be some other explanation of intelligence if it is not found in the dandelion itself. Now if the cause were like the dandelion, it too would have to be explained. There would have to be a cause back of it from which its intelligent acts came since it itself is thought of as not deliberately doing them. Since there can be no cause back of the ultimate cause, the intelligence must be deliberate in itself, which is the same as to say that the cause is conscious of its intelligent actions.

The same may be shown with respect to the moral actions of the first cause. To function morally and also unconsciously would be a contradiction in terms. How can anything be unconsciously moral? How can anything unconsciously do something right or unconsciously do something wrong? We have already shown that a "conscience-act" is a conscious act. Conscience is the moral consciousness that an action is or is not in accord with moral judgment. A bad conscience hurts and a good conscience comforts. But to speak of an unfeeling moral sense or an unconscious conscience is to convey no meaning. A cause which does right and feels no pleasure in it would be unthinkable. It might conceivably do something powerful or wise without having feeling, but we cannot comprehend its doing right without feeling. The very notion of doing right implies conscientiously conforming to the moral judgment. And *conscientiously* conforming to the right is *consciously* conforming to the right. And consciously conforming means that the first cause is a moral Person.

6

Summary and Criticisms of the Theistic Argument

LET US recapitulate, gathering the theistic arguments together and looking at the criticisms of them which have been made. We began our reasoning as follows: Man is a thinking animal. That is fundamental. There is no criticism of the fact which does not assume the fact. No one can say that man is not a thinking animal without thinking. He must rely on thought to deny thought. Thus our minds are our inevitable starting points. There is no going beyond them. There can be no other starting point.

This argument in and of itself is not a theistic argument. But combined with the causal argument, it becomes, we think, a powerful one. That is to say, the inevitability of relying on our own mind proves nothing but that we must rely on our own mind and that there can be no other starting point. But if it can be shown that we are creatures and that God made us, then our observation becomes significant. For if God made us so that thinking is our inevitable source of knowledge, then it would have to be a reliable source of knowledge, a true means of insight into the nature of things.

Now for a summary of the causal argument. We have attempted to show that matter cannot aspire to the role of cause of all things because it needs a cause itself. Nothing in the nature of an effect can be the first cause, for that must be pure or uncaused cause. It must be independent and eternal, for if it depended on anything else it would not be the ultimate cause, and if it came into being in time it would have had to be dependent on something else which brought it into being in time. Then there would have had to be some reason for its coming into being, and this reason must have been its cause so that it could not have been the ultimate cause. We argued, therefore, that there must have been a spiritual first cause, an "unmoved mover."

By the teleological argument we attempted to prove that this universe, as we know it, gives evidence of purpose. And since we had previously noted in the causal argument that the first cause must have been the author of things, this purposiveness must be attributed to that cause. Thus, the cause must be rational or intelligent. Given the first cause and given the fact of the purposiveness of things which have come from this first cause, we are led to the conclusion that the originator of the universe is an intelligent cause.

The moral argument which we presented grew out of our observation of man as he exists in this universe. In addition to being a purposive creature and thereby confirming the purposive character of his creator, he is also a personal, moral creature. His morality, we indicated, could not have come from him himself (though even if it had it must have been from the one who made him himself), but had to have been a natural endowment or, in other words, a creator-implanted characteristic. Since it is inconceivable, we argued, that the creator should implant such a faculty without having it, we concluded that the first and intelligent cause was also moral.

We will now consider some of the objections which have been raised against these proofs. The Scriptures say that "men would not have God in their thinking." This has been nowhere more apparent than in the objections raised against the evidences for the existence of a divine being.

The attack on the ontological argument has usually taken the following form: The fact that man has an idea of God is no proof that there is such a God. The medieval monk Gaunilo observed that he might have an idea of a perfect island but that did not guarantee the existence of such an island. In modern times, Immanuel Kant pointed out that his idea of the presence of certain talers (dollars) in his pocket unfortunately did not assure him that they were actually there. These are essentially rejoinders to the ontological argument as Anselm gave it, though not really adequate replies even to that form of it. Anselm had said that we have an idea of a most perfect being than which none higher can be conceived. He would not have regarded such rejoinders about perfect islands in the sea or dollars in the pocket as relevant, inasmuch as neither of them can be included within the category of "most perfect of existences than which nothing greater can be conceived." Furthermore, if anyone objected to Anselm that he could think of a most perfect being but that that did not guarantee the existence of such a being, Anselm had a ready reply. If, he would say, you have an idea of a most perfect being which does not exist, it is not the most perfect being than which none higher can be conceived. The most perfect being which does exist is higher than the most perfect being which does not exist. Existence, after all, is greater than nonexistence. Therefore, a being which does exist is greater than one which does not exist. Consequently, the most perfect being than which none greater can be conceived must exist, because if it did not exist it would not be the being than which none greater can be conceived.

Thus the usual refutations of the usual form of the ontological argument are not successful. Anselm really had the last
word against most of his opposers through the centuries. But
probably he does not have the last word against all of them.
It still seems to be impossible to prove that God exists simply
on the ground that we have an idea that God exists. Granted
that we do have an idea of a most perfect being than which
none greater can be conceived, how does this prove that such
a being does actually exist? All the argument seems to prove
is that we can have the idea of a most perfect being than
which none greater can be conceived. But that the idea
guarantees that such a being does actually exist we do not
see. If there were indeed such a being, it would be greater
than one which does not exist, just as the idea of such a being
is a greater idea than the idea of a being that does not exist.
But how can more be said? How can this argument prove
more than this—that this being does actually exist?

The Anselmian form of the argument is invulnerable to
most of the supposed refutations of it, but in its most careful
formulation still falls short of demonstration. In any case,
this is not the form of the ontological argument which seems
cogent. The Cartesian form which we have presented may not
properly be called the ontological argument, but be that as it
may, it is not exposed to the criticisms urged against the
classical Anselmian form. Nor have we seen any argument
which refutes it. Indeed we have attempted to show that it is
incapable of refutation because its critic must assume its position in order to attack it.

But some will say, "Granted that we cannot think without
using our thinker, and granted that we did not make ourselves
thinking animals, and granted that if there is a creator he
must have made us this way, and therefore the ontological
argument is in that sense valid; still—and this is the great
objection—what proof do we have that there really *is* any

such first cause as this argument must have to acquire cogency?" In other words, the attack is really mounted against the causal argument to which we now come.

One objection against the causal argument is that it is inconsistent with itself. It rests on the supposition, the criticism goes, that everything must have a cause. On this principle it traces all things back and back to one final cause. And then and there it suddenly stops. But how may it consistently do that? Why does the principle that everything needs a cause suddenly cease to be true? That is, why is it that this so-called first cause does not need a cause? If everything else needs an explanation, why does this not need one? If this does not need an explanation, why do other things need one?

This is not a valid refutation of the causal argument although it is a valid objection to some careless formulations of it. That is, if someone were to say: "Everything must have a cause," this criticism would be completely relevant and telling. The argument, however, is not accurately stated in that manner. It maintains not that everything must have a cause, but that every *effect* must have a cause. Because every effect must have a cause, there must ultimately be one cause that is not an effect but pure cause, or how, indeed, can one explain effects? A cause that is itself an effect would not explain anything but would require another explanation. That, in turn, would require a further explanation, and there would be a deadly infinite regress. But the argument has shown that the universe as we know it is an effect and cannot be self-explanatory; it requires something to explain it which is not, like itself, an effect. There must be an uncaused cause. That point stands.

Immanuel Kant replies that from the line of reasoning which we have followed there must needs be an uncaused cause, a first cause, the author of all effects. Well and good. But, he continues, there is that other line of reasoning which

maintains that this cause itself must have its explanation—
its cause. There is, he says, the thinking that leads to the
infinite regress. Consequently, his position is that this theistic
proof ends in an antinomy, or contradiction, and is therefore
futile. But we have indicated above what is wrong with this
criticism. One part of the antinomy simply is not true. We
grant that if each were true, we would have a contradiction,
and the argument would be futile. But we have shown that
only one line of reasoning is accurate. The notion that there
is an argument for infinite regress is based on the mistaken
supposition that everything must have a cause. There is no
proof for this and we certainly have not appealed to it in the
causal argument. It is, as a matter of fact, an irrelevancy; for
the first cause is, by definition, not an effect at all nor indeed
can be.

The teleological argument has had two main criticisms
urged against it. One is rather technical in character and the
other popular. According to the technical argument, teleol-
ogy pertains only to this world and therefore can tell us
nothing about any cause beyond this world. The popular
argument focuses its attention on the presence of apparently
nonteleological aspects of the universe. That is, there seem
to be many things which do not bear the stamp of purpose;
they are, indeed, quite inconsistent with any purpose and
seem to militate against it.

Kant, again, has been the most redoubtable champion of
the technical objection to the teleological argument. He had a
very distinct preference for this argument among all the theistic proofs. He was much impressed with the "starry skies"
above his head, but they do not, he felt, demonstrate the
existence of purpose beyond this world. It is a transcendental
leap to jump from observations in this world to existences in
the world beyond, he argued.

But, we may ask, what is wrong with the transcendental

leap? If we find things which have no explanation in this world, are we to give up seeking an explanation or are we to look for it elsewhere? Which is more rational, to say there is no explanation or to say that there must be an explanation and to look for it where it may be found? It would seem evident that there must be an explanation either in this world or in another. If it cannot be found in this world, we must conclude that it may be found in another. There seems to be nothing intrinsically irrational in such a conclusion. And if we are proceeding from a finite effect to an infinite cause, what is the fallacy in that? Is it not rather eminently rational to suppose that if a finite cause cannot explain, an infinite cause must?

Then there is the popular objection. So much of the world seems to be nonpurposive. There seems to be so much chance or "happenstance." The sperm fertilizes the ovum, but so many more sperms are used than are needed for the purpose. Hence if purpose is evident in the process, what about these nonpurposive aspects of it? The dandelion seed has a parachute that is eminently adapted for purposes of transportation. Still, many of these seeds land where they cannot germinate. What of them? And speaking of moral purpose, is it not evident that whatever purpose there be in human affairs, the sun does shine on the unjust and disaster does come upon the just? Do not the ungodly often prosper and the godly often suffer?

Let us comment first on the apparent evidence of nonpurposiveness in the natural world. Take the excess of sperms that are "wasted" in the process of fertilization. Note first that if it be so (that is, if they be wasted), that fact does not prove that the one which did fertilize the egg was not so intended. That is, factors which are not evidently purposive do not militate against those which obviously are. As long as it is clear that the sperm which fertilizes the ovum and the dandelion seed that does take root in the earth were adapted for those ends, we have evidence of purpose in the universe. A million instances to the contrary cannot offset this recurring fact.

Second, there is evidence of purpose even in those sperms which do not fertilize the ovum. The situation is such that there are many obstacles to any sperm's reaching the egg. In such a case, what could be more intelligent than to provide many sperms so that one at least is bound to accomplish the purpose? If a man were trying to catch a wild animal that was molesting his neighborhood, it would be considered a mark of intelligence for him to set a number of traps and not just one. Only one would actually be used, but to insure the accomplishment of his purpose he would be wise to set many. Someone may demur at this analogy, saying, "This is true enough of finite man, but God who knows all things cannot be ignorant." But we forget that God is working with finite things. For example, the trapper is finite, and we admit that his action in setting many traps is intelligent. Do we forget that he is God's creation and that God could have made him so that, knowing in advance where the animal would come, he need only to set one trap? If it is no reflection on the intelligence of God to make a man who is less intelligent than He is, would it be a reflection on the purposive intelligence of God to make a sperm that is less intelligent than He is, but which nevertheless is remarkably adapted to its environment?

Finally, we examine the major criticisms of the moral argument. Some grant that there appear to be conscience and morality. They would turn the edge of this admission as an argument for God, however, by saying that it shows nothing about God, but only about a man's own environment. The moral law is no absolute thing, they say; it is merely a reflection of the prevailing mores and traditions of a given community. Conscience varies with the climate; moral law fluctuates with the century; right and wrong are as various as the individuals who profess to know what they are. Such persons will tell me that I write in favor of an absolute conscience and an inflexible moral law because that is what I was taught.

Very well, let us speak to this position. If they say that I write as I do because I have been trained as I have been trained, then I suppose that I may say to them, "You write as you do because you have been trained as you have been trained." And if they take the position they do, not because it is right, but because it happens to be what they were taught was right, then it is not necessarily right after all. That is, they are not necessarily right when they say that I am not necessarily right. They are only reflecting their own provincial backgrounds when they say that I am only reflecting my own provincial background. Their remarks on their own theory are utterly subjective and without validity. Of course, they make them thinking that they are objective and possessing validity. But, when they assume that they are objective, they are assuming our position not their own. In other words, in order to criticize our position they must assume our position. If they are consistent with their own position, they cannot criticize ours or anybody else's. They are obliged to keep a polite silence while the discussion goes on among persons who have reason to believe that there are absolute consciences, rules of right and wrong, universal laws, and other such objective things.

We do not profess to have considered every criticism that has ever been offered against the theistic proofs nor to have said everything that has ever been said in defense, but perhaps enough has been said to justify Paul's words, "The invisible things of him from the creation of the world are clearly seen, being understood by the things that are made" (Rom. 1:20).

PART III

ON THE TRUTH OF CHRISTIANITY

7

The Necessity of Special Revelation

WE HAVE learned a great deal about the Creator of the world. A great deal more remains still to be learned. Indeed, the most important things have not yet been told. Let us gather together what we have discovered, and then consider what we cannot discover without God's making it known.

We do know this much: that we can know no more unless this great Being is pleased to reveal it. He is a personal being, and from our firsthand acquaintance with personal beings we know that they can be known only if they choose to let themselves be known. We may learn some things about any finite person by observing him outwardly, but we cannot certainly know what goes on in his mind and heart unless he takes us into his confidence. One may learn all that there is to know about the clothes men wear without the willing participation of the clothes in the investigations. Not so with the human beings who wear the clothes. They must enter into the study if they are to be studied fully. If this is true of men, how much more so of God? If no one can know me unless I let him, how can anyone hope to know my Creator unless He let him? "For what man knoweth the things of a man, save the

spirit of man which is in him? even so the things of God
knoweth no man, but the Spirit of God" (I Cor. 2:11).

But, coming to the point, what is it that we need still to
know? First, we need to know whether God has made Himself
known. We do know that there is a God. We know that this
God is an intelligent and personal being. Furthermore, we
know that we also exist and are intelligent and personal
beings. We know that we were made in His image, that our
intelligence is but a reflection of His own. We think because
He first thought. Knowing then that He has made us rational
creatures able to think His thoughts after Him, we know that
further revelation to us must be possible. After all, He has
already spoken to us in the things that He has made. What
could prevent Him from speaking to us further? The very
fact that we can raise this question implies that there is a
possible answer. Sticks and stones are not concerned about
divine revelation. They have no ears to hear nor eyes to see.
But we have, and so we ask what we may see and what we may
hear. There is, therefore, a possibility of special revelation.
This much we already know.

But we already know more than this. We know that there
is a probability of revelation. God has already revealed Himself concerning some matters of our destiny. Is it likely that
He would be silent on the matters which matter most? Will
He let us know that He exists only to hide from us any knowledge of how He exists and what are His eternal purposes?
Would He whet our appetite only to starve us? We have not
so learned God. "Seek and ye shall find," seems to be written
large over the universe. Will God set us aseeking so that we
may not find? Would He play such a cruel game?

The world in which we live is a great whodunit. God made
the world but left it for us to find out that He was the Maker.
But there is something unique about this divine whodunit—
the perpetrator wants to be found. He has deliberately left

clues scattered everywhere. He has made His authorship so plain that only the wilfully blind can fail to see. He has not left Himself without a witness, that "haply men might feel after him and find him." He obviously wants to be the known, not the unknown God. We are morally certain that the God of this world would reveal Himself. The only question is where and when has He done it.

In other words, we know of the possibility, and even the high probability, of further revelation. What remains to be known is where that expected revelation is. This, nature does not tell us. It remains yet to be discovered. *That* there must be a further revelation, nature strongly intimates. *What* that revelation is, she cannot say. The book of nature is ended. The second volume, the book of revelation, needs now to be opened.

A second indication of the necessity of special revelation grows out of what we have learned about the nature of God. His holiness we have deduced from the fact of our conscience. This moral faculty, which we traced to Him, assures us that He is not Himself beyond good and evil but much concerned with them. The fact that we feel bad when we violate the conscience and feel good when we act in accord with it convinces us that the author of conscience is on the side of holiness. Through this personal ambassador He smiles on us when we do what is right, and frowns when we transgress the moral law. So we know that God is holy.

But we also have learned that God is merciful. Everything that He has made speaks eloquently of this attribute. To be sure, there are intimations of wrath as well, but they are the exception to the rule. And they do not alter the evidence of His mercy. Does he not make His sun to shine on the unjust? There is vastly more mercy than judgment in this world. That we see, and that we have experienced.

What we do not understand is how these things can be.

How can God be holy and merciful at the same time? We know from nature *that* He is so, but nature does not tell us *how* He can be. Nature reveals that justice and mercy both exist, but it never explains how they kiss each other—how they are reconciled in the same holy person. This is a very acute question and a highly existential one. No idle curiosity drives us on for an answer, but the greatest possible human emergency, even desperation. For this we know: unless these attributes are reconciled, justice will take the precedence. It is self-evident that justice is necessary and equally self-evident that mercy is not. By definition, justice requires that the scales be set in balance. By definition, mercy does not require anything. Justice is necessary; mercy is optional. If any one says that mercy is also necessary, he contradicts himself. A necessary mercy is no mercy; it is justice. If anyone can claim mercy, it is no longer mercy.

Well then, we know that God, being holy and just, will necessarily continue to be holy and just. We do not know that He will continue to be merciful. Where does this leave us? It leaves us trembling. It leaves us certain that God will call us to an account, but utterly uncertain whether He will forgive us anything at all. Nature tells us what God is now doing. What He will do, it neither will nor can tell. It neither preaches to us to flee from the wrath to come, nor to bank on the everlasting mercy. When we want information most desperately, voluable nature is suddenly as silent as the grave. It virtually tells us, "I have said all that I can say. God Himself must now speak if you would know more."

A third need of further revelation arises from nature's witness to the law. Justification by works is revealed in nature. From conscience we discover that we are to do what is right. Such behavior is apparently pleasing to our Maker. On the contrary, doing what is wrong or failing to do what is right, which are the same thing, is displeasing to our Maker. We are acceptable to Him, therefore, only if we do what is right. Good works are essential to our good standing with God. But what of our bad works? It is as clear from nature that they condemn us as that our good ones justify us. What hope is there therefore? Our bad works vitiate our good ones. They cannot be good works if they are corrupted by the presence of bad ones. Yet if we are to be justified, it must be by good works, that is clear. What is not clear, then, is how we are going to be justified. Again, it is also clear from nature that if we are not justified, we must be condemned; for the very works which make our justification impossible make our damnation inevitable. Nature reveals our liabilities, but it has nothing to say of assets. It shows us that we stand condemned, but not how we may be saved.

The preceding is not exactly and completely true. In another sense nature does tell us how to be acceptable to God. To be sure, it is silent about past wrongdoings. However, it does tell us, "This do and thou shalt live." It does stand on the side of the right. It is a preacher of righteousness. "Here is the way, walk ye in it," is its sermon. But a man once said, "I would be willing to be turned into a clock if I could always think what is true and do what is right." What does nature do about the predicament of man—of a creature who knows more than he practices and has more light than he follows? It is well and good for nature to preach righteousness, but what can she do to implement the human will? She has the form of sound words without the power thereof. Nature says to mankind, "Do this and thou shalt live," very much as a cruel person might say to a crippled boy, "Come play with us," or to a shackled slave, "Be free." There is a human bondage which the exhortation, "Be free," does not change. Nature may be the revelation of the condemnation of God, but no one has ever found in her the power of God unto salvation. No, once more the insufficiency of nature is appalling. Just when we need her most, she lapses again into silence. Granted, we say, we must do what is right; but where, O where, do we get the motivation always to do what is right? Nature convinces us that we have a heart of stone, but it does not tell us how we may get a heart of flesh. It shows us that the problem of the soul is the sole of the problem, but it does not explain how to get the new soul. We know by what we learn from nature that we must be born again, but nature herself can only give us the first birth. She can not tell us where to get the second.

A fourth evidence of the necessity of special revelation appears in the problem of human freedom. We have learned from nature that there is an "I" and there is a "He." The I is distinctly and morally and responsibly related to the He. On the other hand, the He is greater than I, since He is author, sustainer, and sovereign over me. It is inconceivable that I should be sovereign over Him, and self-evident that He is sovereign over me. I must do His will, not He, mine. Thus far nature takes us and then suddenly leaves us again. If He is sovereign, we ask of silent nature, how can I be free? If I am free how can He be sovereign? Is His sovereignty an illusion or is my freedom? What shall I choose, his sovereignty, or my own freedom? If I choose His sovereignty, which seems self-evident, how can I continue to be responsible for my own actions? If I choose my own freedom, how can He continue to be sovereign? Once again, this is no idle question but is fraught with the greatest moment for the human soul. For if I deny that He is sovereign, do I not deny Him who is sovereign? But if I deny that I am free, do I not still deny my true and responsible self? I dare not deny either, but how can I affirm both? If it is true that God is sovereign and that I am at the same time free, I need more revelation than nature gives to assure me.

Fifth, natural revelation's insufficiency is seen in its failure to provide any answer to the question of punishment for wrongdoing. That there will be punishment is clear enough, but what it will be nature does not say. If a man die will he live again? Nature does not answer. If he is to be punished in the next world, how intensely and for how long? Nature does not answer.

There will be punishment. There is just enough of it in this world, said Augustine, to show that there will be more in the next, but not enough here to make punishment in the next world unnecessary. Shakespeare, the poet laureate of the human race, bears witness to the uneasiness of the spirit in his famous lines about man's fear of "shuffling off this mortal coil." Through the experience of Lady Macbeth, he reminds us that the cursed spot caused by wrongdoing cannot be erased. Man is a vagabond on the earth, not knowing whence he came nor with certainty where he is going. He knows only that there is a God who hates evil, that he himself has evil deeds on his record, and, worst of all, that the heart from whence they came is evil. That this God not only hates evil but punishes it as well, he knows because his own conscience has no true peace, only foreboding. He dare not be alone with its ominous warnings. He must drown out its prophecies of doom. If he flee from his conscience to the outer world, behold God is there. Nature is red in tooth and claw, and history—much of history—is the story of crime and punishment. *"Die Geschichte der Welt ist das Gericht der Welt."* Whatever a man sows that he must reap, no matter where or in what realm he does the sowing.

Then, in the sixth place, there is the other side of this same coin. If there are punishments, there are also rewards. One is as plain as the other. If it is true that God "will render to every man according to his deeds: . . . unto them that are contentious, and do not obey the truth, but obey unrighteousness, indignation and wrath, tribulation and anguish, upon every soul of man that doeth evil, of the Jew first, and also of the Gentile"—it is also true that "to them who by patient continuance in well doing seek for glory and honour and immortality, eternal life" (Rom. 2:6 ff.). This man knows without revelation. But what he does not know apart from revelation is, how can there be any rewards for sinners? If they escape damnation at all (and that is not at all clear from any testimony of nature), how can they possibly merit any rewards? Man's only hope is mercy, not justice. Justice will only condemn him. Mercy alone can save the evildoer. But, then, if his only hope is mercy, how can there be any rewards? If mercy itself is an unmerited gift, how can it ever merit anything? Yet there will be punishments and there will be rewards. Nature says so. But how these things can be, nature cannot say. We will have to look elsewhere for the answer. The Distributor of rewards and punishments will have to tell us Himself. Nature is mute.

There are many other indications of the necessity of special revelation. We trust that enough have been cited to persuade us that if the really great questions are to be answered, God himself must speak from heaven.

8

The Bible as the Revelation of God (1)

(Internal Proof from Its Answers to Nature's Questions)

THE Bible answers the questions which nature raises. This seems to be an initial presumption in favor of the Bible's being the very word of God, namely, that it answers the questions which only God can answer. So before we consider its inspiration directly, let us observe how it speaks where nature is silent.

First, nature teaches us that there may be and probably is a revelation from God. This is precisely what Scripture claims to be. It makes a perfect fit with nature. Nature reveals God; Scripture confirms the fact that nature reveals God. Nature is an insufficient revelation; Scripture confirms the fact that nature is an insufficient revelation (Rom. chap. 1 and 10). Nature points to the necessity of further revelation; Scripture confirms the fact that nature points to further revelation (Rom. 8:19 ff.). The one thing that nature does not do, Scripture does; namely, it points to itself as the fulfillment of nature.

The Bible claims its own inspiration. More than three

thousand times it claims it. The Bible might conceivably claim to be revelation without being it, but it certainly could not be it without claiming it. While the claim may not be an argument in its favor, the absence of a claim would surely be an argument against it.

Second, the Bible harmonizes the justice and mercy of God. Nature intimates that God is both just and merciful, but it does not explain how this can be. Scripture gives the explanation as well as the affirmation.

It clearly affirms that God possesses each of these attributes in a perfect manner and to an infinite measure. God, it teaches, is perfectly holy (Ex. 15:11; Ps. 30:4; Rom. 1:4). He is so holy that even the holy cherubim cover their faces in His presence, and angels are not chaste in His sight (Isa. 6:1 ff.). He is of purer eyes than to behold iniquity (Hab. 1:13), and without holiness no man shall see Him (Heb. 12:14). Only the pure in heart shall see God (Matt. 5:8). His holiness, furthermore, is immutable. "Shall the judge of all the earth do wrong?" (Ps. 94:2). This for Scripture is a rhetorical question. It is unthinkable that God could do wrong (Rom. 3:4).

At the same time, His mercy endureth forever (Jer. 33:11). It is His perogative to have mercy, and He will have mercy on whom He will have mercy (Rom. 9:15, 18).

Thus the Bible reveals God as so holy that it would seem impossible for Him to be merciful, so merciful that it would seem impossible for Him to be holy. Thus far Scripture goes with nature, though far more deeply than nature was able to probe. Now at the very point where nature becomes silent, Scripture speaks most eloquently. It presents a plan of salvation in which justice and mercy are perfectly harmonized—where they indeed kiss each other. Without detracting in the least from the justice of God by the glorification of His mercy or detracting in the least from the mercy of God by the glorification of His justice, the Bible shows God to be just at the same time that He is the justifier of the ungodly. "Whom God hath set forth to be a propitiation through faith in his blood, to declare his righteousness for the remission of sins that are past, through the forbearance of God; to declare, I say, at this time his righteousness: that he might be just and the justifier of him which believeth in Jesus" (Rom. 3:25,26).

Paul teaches us here of the satisfaction of God's holiness which was made by Christ. He is referring, in the context, to the problem raised by the pardoning of Old Testament saints when no basis for pardon was in evidence. Such pardon might seem to jeopardize the inexorableness of divine justice. Why would God ever pardon sinners as if they had never sinned? Has He changed his implacable, essential hatred of evil? He certainly can not be ignorant of the transgressions of men? Can He have so changed as to love iniquity, or at least to be indifferent to it? What has become of His justice in this situation? Paul is here explaining that Christ was the basis for the pardoning of sinners in the past. It was with respect to the satisfaction which Christ was to make that God reconciled them. But since that sacrifice was not then a fact, it appeared on the surface as if God were proceeding in an unjust manner. Now that in the fullness of times He has set forth Jesus as the propitiation, He has therein declared His righteousness in remitting the sins of former days. Thus, because Christ satisfied the outraged holiness and majesty of God and propitiated it by His perfect sacrifice, God is in a position to pardon without in any way relaxing the demands of His justice. He remains perfectly just while justifying the ungodly—in Christ, who has removed their guilt from them. This is the Christian doctrine of satisfaction, the only theology the world has ever known which has honored the inexorable holiness of God together with His infinite mercy.

Justice and mercy have kissed each other.

Furthermore, Scripture confirms and explains nature's doctrine of justification by works, but in such a way that "he that worketh not" may be justified. This is such a marvelous wisdom that even the angels are represented as standing amazed at its disclosure (Eph. 3:10: "To the intent that now unto the principalities and powers in heavenly places might be known by the church the manifold wisdom of God"). Jesus Christ fulfilled a righteousness for His people. He who knew no sin became sin that we might become the righteousness of God in Him (II Cor. 5:21). He was himself justified in the Spirit but not for Himself alone. He "was delivered up for our offenses, and was raised again for our justification" (Rom. 4:25).

At the same time this justification is no legal fiction. It is not a declaring just what is not really just. It is not a make-believe righteousness, but a real one. That which is declared, is declared because it is so. Christ is identified with His people in a union so intimate that whatever happens to Him happens to them. All His acts are the acts, not of a private, but of a public person. "In Christ shall all be made alive" (I Cor. 15:22). He is the head and they are the members of the same body; what belongs to the head belongs to the body, and what belongs to the body belongs to the head.

We noticed that nature pointed out the need of moral living, but supplied no power for it. So does virtually all religion which has some form of godliness but lacks the power therof. Christianity is itself a moral religion. It is, as a matter of fact, more exacting in its ethical demands than any other religion. Christ insists that if any one is to enter the kingdom of heaven, his righteousness must exceed that of the scribes and Pharisees (Matt. 5:20), which was the righteousness of the generality of ethicists. Their ethics was not wrong in itself, but was not nearly so demanding as Christ is. For example, Jesus teaches: "It is said by them of old time, Thou shalt not kill; and whosoever shall kill shall be in danger of the judgment; But I say unto you, That whosoever is angry with his brother without a cause shall be in danger of the judgment: and whosoever shall say to his brother Raca, shall be in danger of the council: but whosoever shall say, Thou fool, shall be in danger of hell fire" (Matt. 5:21,22). In this He is correcting the prevailing morality of His day, which taught that if men stopped short of murder they had not violated the sixth commandment. Christ, by His three specific instances, none of which gets out of the area of the heart and disposition, teaches that in each case the offender is guilty of murder and in danger of its punishment. And Christ does the same with the other commandments; for example, the seventh, which he shows to be violated by lust alone though it never issue in an overt act of adultery (Matt. 5:28).

Nevertheless, the glory of Christianity is not principally found in its far more exacting code of behavior. In this it differs only in degree from nature and other religions. The utter uniqueness of Christianity lies in the fact that it gives the power to make its more exacting morality come within the range of human achievement. If this were not so, it would remain only a counsel of perfection standing on a grand pedestal of moral excellence; it would never have become the faith which has transformed the lives of millions and set them on the path toward the glorious goal of living.

Christ indicated that He would give what He had commanded, that if what He demanded of His disciples were beyond their power, it was not beyond His power. And He and His Spirit were available to them. "I am the vine, ye are the branches: He that abideth in me, and I in him, the same bringeth forth much fruit: for without me ye can do nothing. . . . If ye abide in me, and my words abide in you, ye shall ask what ye will, and it shall be done unto you"

(John 15:5,7). Paul, testifying to the truth of this great promise in his own experience, later said: "I am crucified with Christ: nevertheless I live; yet not I, but Christ liveth in me: and the life which I now live in the flesh I live by the faith of the Son of God, who loved me, and gave himself for me" (Gal. 2:20). Although "in my flesh dwelleth no good thing" (Rom. 7:18), "I can do all things through Christ which strengthens me" (Phil. 4:13). "What the law could not do, in that it was weak through the flesh, God sending his own Son in the likeness of sinful flesh, and for sin, condemned sin in the flesh: that the righteousness of the law might be fulfilled in us, who walk not after the flesh, but after the Spirit" (Rom. 8:3,4). Paul is saying that the law, or moral code, is impotent, for the nature of man to which it addresses itself is not disposed to obedience. But when the Spirit of Christ comes into the soul, He gives the man an entirely new principle of action which makes him disposed to all that is good and holy and, at the same time, enables him to do that to which he is disposed. Of course, Christianity teaches that the remains of human corruption are in the heart of the Christian, and therefore he does not always, and in perfect degree, work out the grace of God which is in him. But in a measure he does, and in time he will perfectly do so. Thus the atonement of Christ becomes the double cure, cleansing from sin's guilt and power as the familiar hymn says. Samuel Craig in his *Christianity Rightly So Called* (1946) has well observed that Christianity views the sinner very much as a criminal who is condemned to capital punishment and at the same time is dying of a mortal disease. For a person in this double difficulty, two things must be done. If the governor should grant a pardon, it would do no good for the man will die of his disease. On the other hand, if a physician should effect a cure, that would do no good for the man will die at the hands of the state. He must be given a pardon and a cure at the same time. This Christianity does for the corrupted and condemned sinner. Nature could show that it had to be done, but nature could in no wise do it.

The Bible's contribution to the freedom-sovereignty problem is quite different from its contribution to the justice-mercy problem. The latter, it truly solves. But the former it does not solve. Rather, it simply proves that freedom and sovereignty are both true, giving irrefutable evidence in support of each. When we came from the classroom of nature, we understood that she was teaching that each of these apparently conflicting truths is so, but we wondered whether such a doctrine could be accepted. The fact that we could not fully understand them was no argument against them—that we knew, for our inability to understand fully was characteristic of a great many things which we nevertheless knew to be true. Still this antimony was so practical and vital that we hesitated to accept it on the word of nature alone. The Bible confirms the teaching of nature and by its much fuller revelation of God and man shows that each truth is true of each person. God is sovereign and man is free.

The Word of God makes many declarations about the sovereignty of God. He brings His will to pass in all the earth (Eph. 1:9). Who is this, the prophet asks, who says that anything comes to pass and "the Lord commandeth it not"? (Lam. 3:37) In a certain sense, God is the ordainer of evil as well as of good, and He makes the wicked for the day of evil (Isa. 45:7, Prov. 16:4). He knows all things from the beginning, and not a sparrow falls to the ground without His knowledge (Acts 15:18, Matt. 10:29). He controls the fate of men and nations (Prov. 8:15).

At the same time, man is utterly free and completely responsible for all his actions. Offenses must come, says Christ, "but woe to that man by whom the offence cometh" (Matt. 18:7). Christ's death was foreordained from the beginning, but at the same time those who crucified him were guilty of His death (Acts 2:23). Likewise John the Baptist was the Elijah who had been predicted, and when he came, men did to him "whatsoever they listed, as it is written of him" (Mark 9:13).

The Bible, therefore, leaves this unmistakable inference: God brings His will to pass to the last detail, but at the same time He does so without the least violation of the will of any creature. How can this be, the Bible does not tell us, probably because we could not understand it if it did. But that it is so, we are assured. So we go on our way confident that the God of heaven and earth is indeed the great sovereign we have been led to believe Him to be, but at the same time we do so with the full assurance that we are the free moral agents that we have always known ourselves to be.

Again, nature reveals that there is now, and probably will be, punishment but knows not when, where, or how it will be. The Bible confirms nature and answers the questions she poses. "The wages of sin is death" (Rom. 6:23). This expression, set in antithesis to eternal life, signifies eternal death. The punishment begins immediately at death (Heb. 9:27) and continues during the intermediate state prior to the resurrection, during which period the souls of the wicked, though disembodied, are exquisitely miserable (Luke 16:19 ff.) This judgment is private, individual, and spiritual. The "day of judgment" or final judgment will follow the resurrection; it will be public and will issue in the condemnation of devils and men (Matt. 25:31 ff.). The misery of men under divine judgment will be beyond the power of the mind to conceive or the body to endure (Ps. 90:11). It will be punishment in body and in soul (Matt. 10:28) without mitigation (Matt. 5:26). Though perfectly terrible in every instance, it will be yet more terrible in proportion to the number and gravity of sins done in this life (Matt. 5:22). It will be without cessation, forever (Mark 9:44 f.). If men in this life live under constant fear of death (Heb. 2:15), the Bible more than confirms that fear. The half has not been told by nature. "All this," the Bible says to sinful man, "and hell too."

With respect to the problem of rewards in a theology of mercy, the Bible gives the answer. It emphasizes throughout that "to him that worketh not, but believeth on him that justifieth the ungodly, his faith is counted for righteousness" (Rom. 4:5). Salvation is by faith that it may be of grace (Rom. 4:16). The publican who could claim nothing but merely threw himself on the sheer mercy of God went down to his house "justified" (Luke 18:9 ff.). At the same time, the Bible speaks often of "rewards" (Matt. 5:12; Luke 6:23; Col. 2:18). They are, however, the rewards of grace not merit. They are gracious gifts as much as justifying grace is. There is no merit in anything that any man does, the gospel says (Luke 17:10). Jesus tells a parable of a man whose servant, after he had worked in the fields, came into the house and continued to serve the master. "But which of you, having a servant plowing or feeding cattle, will say unto him by and by, when he is come from the field, Go and sit down to meat? And will not rather say unto him, Make ready wherewith I may sup, and gird thyself, and serve me, till I have eaten and drunken; and afterward thou shalt eat and drink? Doth he thank that servant because he did the things that were commanded him? I trow not" (Luke 17:7-9). Christ's point was clear enough to the self-righteous Pharisees. Nothing anyone does deserves thanks. All that men do in obedience to God is merely their duty. Perfect obedience is minimal duty. Merit is utterly excluded. On the other hand, Christ taught that even a cup of cold water, given in his name, would not lose its "reward" (Mark 9:41). In other words, Christ is disposed graciously to acknowledge the least things which his people do out of affection for him, although the utmost that they do deserves nothing. If they were perfect they would deserve nothing, but though they may be imperfect, they will receive a gracious recognition. In this way the Bible consistently combines two conceptions which, on the surface, seem altogether incompatible.

We have noted earlier that the Bible claims to be the Word of God. The answers which it, and it alone, gives to the great questions left unanswered by nature, tend to suggest that the two books had the same author. Or perhaps we should think of a text book, the first part of which states the problems and the latter part, the solutions. The first book would be incomplete without the second, and the second could not be appreciated without the first. Together they constitute one book of God in two parts: natural and special revelation.

So there is a wonderful unity between nature and revelation in the one book of God. But revelation itself reveals a remarkable internal unity. If it is true that the created world is a cosmos or ordered whole or universe, it is not less apparent that the Bible is one book. It has sixty-six books but it is yet one book.

This is more remarkable than the unity of the book of nature. For when God wrote the book of nature, He did it by Himself alone. " 'Let there be'," He said, "and there was." But when He wrote the book of Scripture, He did not do it by Himself alone. He used human instrumentality. And not one man, but about forty men over many centuries.

The men He used were living, thinking, feeling men. If he had put them in a trance or rendered them unconscious or simply overpowered them, His Word would have been equally infallible, but neither so interesting nor so remarkable.

9

The Bible as the Revelation of God (2)

(External Proof from the Authority of Christ)

THUS far we have found reason for believing that back of the universe, including ourselves, is an uncreated, independent, unlimited, eternal, wise, holy, and self-conscious Person. There has been only one human being who dared to say, "He that hath seen me hath seen the Father." Since He made such a claim and since millions of persons believe that claim, He is entitled to some consideration by us. We will approach the subject of Christ as noncommitally as possible. We will be prejudiced neither in its favor nor against it, but will simply consider it and follow where it appears to lead.

I had a very interesting professor at Harvard University who used to attempt to introduce his classes to Christ. In attendance he would have, in addition to the men of the divinity school, a number of the regular university students who were often totally ignorant of Christ. This fact, so far from dismaying the professor, rather pleased him, for from these students he used to like to get what he called "the virgin reaction" to Jesus. The theological students, having been acquainted with Jesus before, could only afford the philosophy of the second glance. But Dr. H. J. Cadbury, who himself had studied the texts hundreds of times, could always learn something from those who gave the fresh response of the newly introduced. Let us attempt to put ourselves in the position of these students and try to experience the initial response to Jesus Christ.

When we read the accounts of Jesus, we instinctively recognize here the perfect man. Matthew describes One whom we see to be the ideal Jew; Mark, the ideal Roman; John, the ideal Son of God; and Luke, the universal ideal who is man's ideal and God's as well. And every man who approaches Christ seems to feel the same thing—He is the ideal of that man. To the artist He is the one altogether lovely. To the educator He is the master teacher. To the philosopher He is the wisdom of God. To the lonely He is a brother; to the sorrowful, a comforter; to the bereaved, the resurrection and the life. And to the sinner He is the Lamb of God that taketh away the sin of the world.

"No one," says Watson, "has yet discovered the word Jesus ought to have said, none suggested the better word he might have said. No action of his has shocked our moral sense. None has fallen short of the ideal. He is full of surprises, but they are all the surprises of perfection. You are never amazed one day by his greatness the next by his littleness. You are quite amazed that he is incomparably better than you could have expected. He is tender without being weak, strong without being coarse, holy without being servile. He has conviction without intolerance, enthusiasm without fanaticism, holiness without Pharisaism, passion without prejudice. This man alone never made a false step, never struck a jarring note. His life alone moved on those high levels where local limitations are transcended and the absolute Law of Moral Beauty prevails. It was life at its highest."

The virgin reaction and all the subsequent reactions of the world to Jesus Christ is, then, that He is the ideal, the perfect man, the moral paragon of the race. I do not wish to gloss over the fact that not absolutely everyone has agreed with this verdict. I know that George Bernard Shaw spoke of a time in Christ's life when, as he said, Christ was not a Christian. I know that some have thought that Socrates died more nobly than Jesus; that others believe Him to have been morally surpassed. But the overwhelming testimony of the world is to the perfection, the incomparable perfection, of Jesus of Nazareth. The few exceptions could easily be shown to rest on fundamental misconceptions of certain things which Jesus said or did; and, furthermore, the vast majority of those who do take exception usually think that some imagined fault is a failure of Christ to be, as George Bernard Shaw said, a Christian! They seem to know of no higher standard by which to test Christ than the standard of Christ Himself.

But now we find ourselves in an extraordinary situation. If we admit, as the world does, that Christ is the perfect man, we must then admit that He is also God! Why, you ask, if we acknowledge Christ to be the perfect man, must we then acknowledge Him to be God also? Is there not a great difference between man and God—even between perfect man and God? Why should the admission of the one require the admission of the other? Why must the perfect man be God? Because the perfect man says He is God. And if He is not God, then neither can He be a perfect man. We despise Father Divine as a man for claiming to be God, which we know he is not. If Jesus Christ is not God, we must depise Him also, for He claims far more clearly than Father Divine that He is God. We must, therefore, either worship Christ as God or despise or pity Him as a man.

Just a minute, you say, what proof do we have that Jesus

Christ ever claimed to be God? My answer is that we have overwhelming evidence that He entertained this high opinion of Himself. This, for example, is what He says of Himself:

"I and the Father are one";

"No man cometh to the Father but by me";

"He that hath seen me hath seen the Father";

"Before Abraham was I am";

"Are thou the Son of God," the high priest asked; "Thou hast said," was Christ's reply;

"Baptize," he commanded, "in the name of the Father, and of the Son, and of the Holy Ghost";

"Whom do ye say that I, the Son of Man, am?" he asked his disciples. "Thou art the Christ, the son of the living God," Peter replied.

"Blessed art thou Simon Bar-jona: for flesh and blood hath not revealed this unto thee, but my Father which is in heaven," he said.

Well, you say, is this not a characteristic way for religious teachers to speak, to make these grandiose statements? It is true that Bronson Alcott once said to a friend, "Today I feel that I could say, as Christ did, I and the Father are one." "Yes," the other replied, "but the difference is this: Christ got the world to believe him." To be sure, a certain man, formerly from Brooklyn, then Harlem, now Philadelphia, accepts divine honors and worship; but outside his little clientele he is the laughing stock of the world.

It is significant that not one recognized religious leader in the history of the world has ever laid claim to be God except Jesus. Moses did not. Paul was horrified when people tried to worship him. Mohammed insisted he was merely a prophet of Allah. Buddha did not even believe in the existence of a personal God, and Confucius was skeptical. Zoroaster was a worshiper but was not worshiped. We repeat—of the recognized religious leaders of all time, Jesus of Nazareth, and Jesus of Nazareth alone, claimed to be eternal God.

It is not merely that Jesus on various occasions definitely affirmed His deity; what is perhaps more telling still is that He always assumed it. The Sermon on the Mount, for example, is regarded as predominantly moral instruction. No heavy theology here, they say. This is Christ telling us what we are to do, not what we are to believe about Him. Not directly, perhaps, but indirectly He says a great deal about Himself and lays impressive incidental claim to His divinity.

Note these six distinct pointers to His supernatural being in this one sermon on Christian morality (Matt. 5-7). First, He declares with absolute authority who shall and who shall not inherit the kingdom of God (the Beatitudes). If I, for example, said anything like that on my own authority, you would smile pityingly or frown. He said, secondly, that the prophets, who suffered and died centuries before, were persecuted "for my sake." Suppose that I said that Martin Luther suffered for my sake, what would you think about me? Third, "but I say unto you" is the constant refrain through this sermon by which He assumes His right to speak with the authority of the word of God on which He is commenting. Fourth, He says that in the last judgment some will say to Him, "Lord, Lord," but He shall say to them, "depart from me; I never knew you." Fifth, the sermon concludes with the parable of the two houses, one built on sand and the other on a rock, one to fall and one to stand. And what is this rock? His teaching. Finally, the people themselves, sensed the supreme dignity of this teacher, for they said, "He spoke as one having authority, and not as the scribes."

What did Jesus' contemporaries think of Him? Some, to be sure, said He was possessed of a devil. But the others? "Behold the man," said Pilate. "Surely this was a son of God," said the centurion who watched Him die. "Never man so spake," the people said. "Behold the Lamb of God," was the testimony of John the Baptist, whom all men recognized as a prophet. "My Lord, and my God," said doubting Thomas. The disciples were standing near Caesarea Philippi—a city built in honor of Caesar, who was claiming divine honors, not far from the grotto to Pan, whom many worshiped as the god of nature—when Jesus asked them who they thought He was. "Thou are the Christ," declared Peter, "the son of the living God." John said of Him, "We beheld his glory, the glory as of the only begotten, full of grace and truth." And Paul adored Him with a most abundant variety of expressions as his great God and Saviour Jesus Christ. For example, the one expression "unsearchable riches of Christ" occurs thirteen times in his epistles. What does Paul mean by the "unsearchable riches of Christ"? It is impossible to put enough meaning into the expression to do justice to the feeling of the Apostle. Rendell Harris, attempting to translate this expression in Eph. 3:8, threw up his hands in despair and cried, "The unexplorable wealth of Christ!"

We are fully aware that to attribute Godhood to any man is a colossal affirmation. It borders on the incredible, the impossible. But when we consider the impression of His perfect humanity, the great claims He made for Himself in the most humble possible way, the unrestrained adoration and worship of those who knew Him, the miracles associated with Him whose life was a "blaze of miracle," and the constantly recurring miracles of grace which have attended the heralding of His name throughout the world, we protest that no matter how difficult it may be to believe that a man was also God, it is impossible to deny it of Christ. If it is difficult to believe, it is impossible to doubt.

Some things pertaining to Christ which we have merely mentioned in this general survey, we will consider more particularly in the following chapters. The miracles He performed, prophecies which He fulfilled, the influence He has exerted on individuals and institutions, and the fact of Christian experience will all receive a closer look.

The reader may well ask, "What is the bearing of all this on the inspiration of the Bible? Granted that Christ is the Son of God, what does that tell us about the Word of God, or how does it prove that the Bible is the Word of God?" It may seem at first glance as if we have digressed from our subject. Such, however, is not the case. Actually, the deity of Christ is the strongest of all arguments for the inspiration of the Bible simply because this Christ certifies that the Bible is inspired, and if He is the Son of God He is incapable of error. Men may make mistakes; God cannot. If God says the Bible is His Word, it must be so. There can be no stronger evidence. This fact is infinitely superior to all other considerations.

"But wait," says every keen observer, "this is circular reasoning of the most obvious sort." And we admit that, at first glance, our reasoning does seem exposed to just this criticism, which, if it is valid, demolishes the whole argument. If the stricture stands, the reasoning must fall, and what appeared to be an argument of infinite force will actually have no force at all.

If, however, we look again, we shall perhaps see that there is no circularity in the reasoning. We are not arguing from the authority of the Bible to the authority of Christ and from thence to the authority of the Bible. If we were, we would be in a vicious and futile circle. We do not beg the question by beginning with the assumption that the Bible is inspired, proceed to prove from that that Christ is divine, and then return fortified by His authority to prove that the Bible is inspired. Rather, we begin with the Bible without assuming its inspiration. This is the very point in question, and we do not beg it at the outset. We begin with the Bible, not as inspired, but merely as a trustworthy document historically speaking.

Nor is there any reason to apologize for assuming the basic trustworthiness of the New Testament records. There was a time when they were challenged, but that time is long and permanently past. The Bible has been the most studied book in the world, the New Testament has been more studied than the Old, and the three purely historical accounts of the life of Jesus (Matthew, Mark, and Luke) have received more attention than any other part of the New Testament. So we may say that the historical life of Jesus has been the most studied single topic in the history of research. Out of the mass of critical studies by conservative, liberal, and radical scholars, there has come an overwhelming consensus that the Synoptic records give us the most authentic ancient history extant in the world. This is the opinion, not only of those who worship the Christ to whom these records bear witness, but also the testimony of those who do not. They may question whether Jesus is indeed the Son of God (and books such as this are written for the purpose of discussing that question), but they leave no doubt that we have an essentially accurate account of His life on earth. For our purposes that is all that is necessary. It gives us a sure historical foundation on which to rest our discussion. We know there was such a person as Jesus and that He said and did essentially the things attributed to Him. Our question then is, "Who was He, and may we believe in Him?" We have, in the preceding pages, attempted to show that beginning with the historical Jesus we are led unmistakably to the divine Jesus.

There remains to be shown only that Christ did teach that the Bible was the inspired Word of God. He tells us the law of God is so sacred that not one jot or one tittle is unessential. "For verily I say unto you, Till heaven and earth pass, one jot or one tittle shall in no wise pass from the law, till all be fulfilled" (Matt. 5:18). This word cannot be broken (John 10:35); on the contrary, all that is written must be fulfilled (Matt. 26:24). Christ had his quarrels with the Pharisees about the interpretation of Scripture but not about its status as inspired. "It is written," as a sign of the infallible word, was a formula with Him as with them. As a matter of fact, when He engaged in controversy with them, He would make his argument rest on a single word of the sacred text (John 10:34). The evidence that Christ did regard the Old Testament Scripture as inspired is so pervasive that it is seldom contested today even by those who themselves do not accept this inspiration but think that Jesus was mistaken, a victim of the "errors" of his day.

But what of the New Testament? Christ's Bible was the Old Testament, not the New. Is there any ground in the teaching of Jesus for supposing that He gave it His imprimatur? Admittedly, the evidence is more inferential and less explicit than is His testimony to the Old Testament.

First of all, there is the consideration of probability. Is it at all likely that God would have inspired the Old Testament, which was merely preparatory to the coming of Jesus, and then leave His own life and the exposition of its meaning to uninspired men? It is not like God to make the second dispensation poorer than the first. Furthermore, if we need the preparation of the many books of the Old Testament in order to appreciate Christ, surely we need an authoritative exposition of the great life for which they prepare us. If we had no other argument for the inspiration of a sequel to the Old Testament, this would seem to justify our conviction that there must be one.

But in addition to the inferential argument just mentioned, we have the explicit statement of Jesus himself that He would lead His disciples into all truth, including, presumably, the many thing He desired to tell them which they were not able at that time to bear (John 14:26; 15:26; 16:12,13). So we know that Jesus intimated that there was to be further revelation since He was not Himself able to complete what He had begun.

The question remains, how do we know that the New Testament is the answer to that intimation? We know it because the New Testament was written by the authenticated messengers of Christ, namely, the Apostles. They were sent out by Christ and given His very powers over disease and devils. Since they claim to have been sent and authorized by Christ and to have received His revelations (Mark 3:14 f.; 6:7 f; Luke 9:1 ff.; Acts 1:3,15 ff.; 2:1 ff.; 9:1 ff.; II Cor. 12:1 ff.; Gal. 1:12 *passim*), they are to be believed if Christ is to be believed.

So the question remaining is, is it clear that the Apostles wrote the New Testament? Yes, the entire New Testament was written by Apostles or apostolically sanctioned men (Mark carrying the endorsement of Peter, and Luke, that of Paul). We may say, therefore, that the New Testament was written by the authorized and supernaturally endowed representatives of Christ or their appointees. And consequently it carries the same imprimatur as the Old Testament: Jesus Christ.

Let us sum up the matter by saying that the entire Bible carries the certification of the Son of God which brings with it infallible authority. Thus the written Word of God has the seal of the living word of God.

10

Miracles of the Bible (1)

CONCERNING miracles there are two important questions to be asked. First, what is the evidence for miracles and, second, what is their evidential value? If there is to be any argument from miracles, there must first be clear evidence that they actually occur.

Before we proceed to consider the evidence for miracles, let us ask ourselves whether there can be any such evidence. This is a rather absurd question, we grant, but we must consider it. Many persons never face the question at all because they rule out the possibility of miracles before they consider any actual evidence for them. One of the most outstanding Biblical scholars in the country once said publicly, in answer to a question concerning his interpretation of miracles in the Old Testament, "When I meet an alleged miracle, I simply treat it as legend." This scholar no doubt would not bother reading this chapter or anything like it. He knows in advance that any and all alleged miracles are legends merely. But how does he know it? He does not know it; he merely declares it. However, there are more philosophically minded thinkers who would say that this professor is right in his conclusion but wrong in the way he arrives at it. They agree that there is no such thing as miracles and that records of them must be legends of some sort. But these men attempt to prove their statement and not merely to assert it arbitrarily.

Some would offset the evidential power of miracles by claiming that there never could be enough proof of a miracle in the face of the overwhelming evidence of natural law against it. David Hume once argued that there is more evidence for regularity in nature than for irregularity (supernaturalism); therefore, regularity and not irregularity must be the truth of the matter. The argument is palpably unsound, indeed irrelevant. Certainly there is more evidence for the regular occurrence of nature than there ever could be for any supernatural occurrence. But the argument for miracle is not meant to be an argument against the regularity of nature. It is merely an argument against the regularity of nature in every particular instance. Indeed the argument for miracle rests on the regularity of nature generally. There is no such thing as supernatural events except as they are seen in relation to the natural. And they would not be extraordinary if there were no ordinary against which background they are seen. They could not be signs of anything if they were not different from the *status quo*. When one argues for the occasional miracle, he is in the same breath arguing for the usually nonmiraculous. If all nature became supernatural, there would be no room for miracle; nothing would be miracle because all would be miracle.

At the same time, all the evidence that there is for the regularity of nature generally is no argument at all against the occasional miracle. Such evidence simply argues for the fact that the normal course of nature is natural. It does not rule out or in, for that matter, the possibility that the irregular may happen. It only proves that as long as there is nothing but nature to take into consideration, there will probably be no deviation from the order with which we have become familiar. If there be a God, all the evidence of an undeviating nature from its creation to the present moment does not provide the slightest certainty that nature will continue the same way another moment. The same God who made it and preserved it in the present pattern for so long may have fulfilled His purpose in so doing and may proceed immediately, this moment, to do otherwise than in the past. Only if the evidence for the regularity of nature were somehow to show that there is no being outside nature who can in any way alter it, can there be an argument against the possibility of miracles. But this the evidence does not do, does not purport to do, cannot do. Therefore it can never be regarded as an argument against miracle. In the strictest sense Hume's objection is irrelevant.

What is the relation of unpredictability in modern physics to the notion of miracle? Certainly the universe is no longer thought to be fixed in the sense that it once was. The quantum theory has satisfied most physicists that there is such a thing as indeterminism, or unpredictable behavior in the laws of nature. As Bertrand Russell has remarked, while psychology in our time has become more deterministic, physics has become less so. Some have utilized the concept of indeterminacy in nature as a wedge for miracle. Having felt fenced in by the arguments based on the regularity of nature, they have welcomed this apparent avenue of escape by which they may remain scientific and still affirm miracle. Indeterminacy runs interference for the power of God, or more piously we should say, makes it possible to believe that God may act miraculously inasmuch as He acts indeterministically in created nature.

So far as we can see, the situation for the credibility of miracle is neither improved nor worsened by indeterminacy.

For one thing, indeterminacy is hardly a proven concept. Or more precisely, it would seem more likely that man cannot in every case determine the laws by which nature operates, than that she herself is indeterministic. It is conceivable that in the area of quantum physics no less than elsewhere nature is deterministic, and what is undetermined are the laws of her behavior. Nature may be determined, but man has not determined how. If this is the case, the to-do about indeterminism is wasted mental effort.

If nature herself is indeterministic, then what? Then it still would remain highly unlikely that an indetermism in nature could explain why once and only once, thousands of years ago, a man walked on water, but no one else has been able to do so before or since. Presumably the indeterminism of nature could never be employed to account for such a unique phenomenon. Furthermore, if this is the explanation, Christ Himself was deceived. He should have been surprised to be around at the one moment when nature was behaving differently from all previous times. He should have been as much amazed as the others, unless (and here is the hopeless supposition) He were a downright sophisticated fraud who took advantage of the most unbelievable opportunity that the world could imagine. Furthermore, there is the matter of His actual predictions, which would be rendered impossible in an indeterministic universe.

Some would affirm the *a priori* impossibility of miracles because of the nonexistence of God. They rightly state that a miracle to have meaning must be the work of an intelligent, powerful, and purposive divine being. In this we go along with them. Then they say that since there is no such being as this, there can be no such thing as miracle. And we agree with that. If it can be shown that there is no God, it will also be shown in the same effort that there is no miracle. What do the opponents of a personal God set forward against His existence? We have already attempted to show in other parts of this book some of the arguments for the existence of God and in so doing have incidentally considered and shown the inadequacy of the arguments against His existence. We need not reconsider them here. Sufficient to say now that we are confident the arguments against the divine existence are not sound, and therefore this argument against miracles falls with them.

.What is the positive evidence that miracles have occurred? A discussion of this subject with any degree of fullness would require an entire volume itself. We must delimit the field. And so we will consider here only the miracles of Jesus Christ.

Everyone knows that the gospel narratives tell of a large number of miracles that were performed by Christ. A great many more are alluded to but not related. This is so generally known that I feel perfectly safe in assuming the readers' acquaintance with the accounts of Christ's healing the sick, opening the eyes of the blind, raising the dead, walking on water, multiplying a boy's lunch to feed more than five thousand hungry persons, and a host of other such deeds.

No one disputes the fact that the gospel accounts tell of Jesus Christ's performing miracles. There have been attempted naturalistic explanations, to be sure, but so far as we know no one has attempted the job of showing that all accounts of the apparently miraculous are merely accounts of natural events which were misconstrued by the writer or reader. For example, who would care to show that John's report of Thomas' placing his fingers in the side of the resurrected Christ to feel His former wounds was not meant to present an essentially supernatural event, namely, physical resurrection? Persons may or may not believe what John says, but how can they doubt that John presents them as happening? As even naturalistic New Testament critics usually say, there is no doubt that the early Christians believed these supernatural things did occur.

If it be granted that the biographers of Christ say He wrought miracles, the only questions remaining are: can these writers be believed? and if so, what do the miracles prove?

Can these writers be believed when they relate that Christ wrought supernatural deeds or miracles? Well, why not? People are assumed to be reliable in their relating of events unless there is some reason for thinking that they are not so. What reason is there for thinking that these writers are not reliable? So far as they are known, they have the reputation of honesty. Was there some bias present which would have tended to corrupt their honesty in the case of these miracles? There is no evidence of bribery by money or position. Their reporting of miracles as vindications of Jesus did not bring them into good standing with the powers in their own community. It caused Peter and John to be imprisoned and all the apostles to be brought into disfavor with most of the Jewish community. It stands to reason that a person cannot advance his own worldly interests by championing a person condemned by law and executed as a criminal.

But what about their other-worldly interests? Is it possible that these men believed that by shading the truth and relating what did not occur they would thereby gain an interest in heaven? Did they think that because of their lying about "miracles," Jesus would own them in the next world? Merely to ask this question dispels it. The whole picture of Jesus is that of a teacher of righteousness who required His disciples to make righteous judgments and speak the truth which alone could make free. It would not seem reasonable to believe that they could have thought they would please Jesus by telling lies about Him and actually earn His praise in the world of perfect righteousness to come.

Or could they have been sentimentalists? That is, could they have supposed that by telling what they knew to be untrue, they could nevertheless do good? Could they have felt that if people could be persuaded that this Jesus was a supernatural being with supernatural powers, they would then obey Him and walk in paths of righteousness? Could they have supposed that by doing evil this great good would come? Is it possible that they, knowing there were no miracles, were nonetheless willing to follow Christ to the death, but that others would need the help of such superstition?

There is an insuperable objection to this "pious fraud" idea. As we have already mentioned, Christ himself is depicted as a teacher of strict truth and righteousness. If the disciples had told deliberate and huge falsehoods, their very zeal would have lead them into the grossest kind of disobedience. They would also have known that their own souls were in peril, for Christ had said that a good tree brings forth good fruit and that He would say to liars in the last day, "I never knew you; depart from me, ye that work iniquity" (Matt. 7:22, 23). "If you love me," Christ had said, "keep my commandments." It seems incredible that the disciples in their very zeal for Jesus would zealously disobey His commandments, that in their desire to be with Him and advance His cause they would seal their own doom.

So much for the inherent improbability of such a course on the part of the disciples. But there is equally great difficulty in the external situation. Even if it were conceivable that the disciples so forgot their Master's teachings and their own spiritual interest as to violate thus grossly His canons of righteousness, it does not at all follow that those to whom they addressed themselves stood to be deceived. After all, the disciples would have foisted these "pious frauds" upon those among whom they were supposed to have been done. They would have told the very people who were supposed to have been present on the occasion, the fiction that Jesus fed five thousand. They would have told the people of Cana themselves that Christ turned water to wine at a feast in their small community, which everybody in that community would immediately deny ever took place there. The "pious fraud" idea, even if it were psychologically thinkable, could be historically thinkable only if it were perpetrated in a different land at a different time. But that in the same generation these things could have been preached as having occurred among the very people who knew that they had not occurred is hardly credible.

11

Miracles of the Bible (2)

IN THE preceding chapter we discussed the miracles of Christ and concluded by stressing the fact that they were reported to the very people among whom they supposedly had been done. Although the witnesses of these events might have got away with such reports among highly credulous strangers who knew nothing about the events in question, they could never have deceived the very people among whom the miracles were supposed to have taken place. It would therefore seem impossible to impeach the honesty of the witnesses. All the factors actually favor their honesty, which must be assumed in the first instance unless there is some reason for questioning it. But when we examine any possible reasons, we find none. Candor requires that their record be received as a record of what they thought took place.

But the question still remains whether what they thought took place did actually take place. Granted that they meant to tell the truth, did they succeed in their honest intention? With the best of intentions men have often been grossly mistaken. Is it not possible that these writers were similarly mistaken? In other words, there remains the question of the competency of the witnesses.

We note, in the first place, that they had the best possible jury to test their competency—their own contemporaries among whom the events related were said to have taken place. If the writers had been palpably contradicted by the facts, the people to whom they related the facts would have been the very ones to expose them. If they had been misguided zealots, the nonzealots to whom they spoke could have spotted it in a moment and repudiated it as quickly. If they had garbled the actual events, eyewitnesses in quantity could have testified to the contrary. If these historians had actually been bigoted, benighted fanatics with no historical sense, incapable of distinguishing between fact and fancy, between occurrences in external nature and in their own imagination, thousands of Israelites could have made that very clear.

As a matter of fact, their record went unchallenged. No man called them liars; none controverted their story. Those who least believed in Jesus did not dispute the claims to His supernatural power. The apostles were imprisoned for speaking about the resurrection of Christ, not, however, on the ground that what they said was untrue, but that it was unsettling to the people. They were accused of being heretical, deluded, illegal, un-Jewish, but they were not accused of being inaccurate. And that would have been by far the easiest to prove if it had been thought to be true.

Actually, the Israelites of Jesus' own day, so far from denying His miraculous power, admitted it. They not only admitted it, but they used it against Him. Precisely because He did miracles, they condemned Him. That is, they attributed the miracles, which they admitted He did, to the power of the devil (Matt. 12:24). We are not here concerned with the accusation but with the incidental admission. What we are concerned with here is that hostile contemporary leaders freely admitted that Jesus' miracles were true, however evil they held their origin to be. The fact they did not dispute, only the interpretation of it. The witness they did not question. The competency of the writers was not doubted by the very generation which alone could have challenged it. It seems highly irrelevant, on historical grounds, for subsequent generations to raise such questions when the generation in which the events are said to have occurred did not do so. Later generations may object on philosophical grounds or argue *a priori* that these things could not have happened. Those arguments have to be met on their own grounds as we have attempted to do. But the historicity of certain events cannot be questioned by people who were not there when they were not questioned by the people who were there. We may or may not agree with the Pharisees' interpretation that Christ did His works by Satan's power, but we are in no position to contest the Pharisees' knowledge of what He did. They were there and we were not.

This corroborative testimony of contemporaries, friends, and, especially, enemies, is the main vindication of the competency of the gospel witnesses. But there is also the feasibility of the documents themselves. These miracles are not fantastic things such as those recorded in the apocryphal accounts of Jesus. They are of a piece with the character of Jesus Himself—benign, instructive, redemptive. He Himself was a special and unique person; it is not surprising that He had special and unique powers. Indeed, it would be more surprising if He had not had them. Never man so spake, never man so lived, never man so loved, never man so acted. As Karl Adam has said, Jesus' life was a blaze of miracle. Miracles were as natural to Him as they would be unnatural to other men. He was a true man indeed, but He was no ordinary man. Miracles are surprising when attributed to other men; it would appear surprising if they had not been associated with this man.

Some have asked whether the miracles may not be naturally explained as the result of Christ's unusual knowledge and understanding of the laws of nature. May He not have possessed some occult acquaintance with the secrets of nature that enabled Him to unleash certain of her powers in a perfectly natural manner, however supernatural it may have appeared to those unfamiliar with these esoteric laws?

To this there are several negative replies. For one thing there is a moral objection. Jesus himself referred to His works or allowed others to refer to them as evidence of His supernatural power. It would have been palpable dishonesty to do so if He had known all the time that He was merely exerting secret, but natural, power. Thus He asked His disciples, if they could not believe Him for His words' sake, to believe him for His works' sake (John 14:11). He reassured the doubting John the Baptist of the reality of His Messianic calling by appealing to the miracles He wrought (Matt. 11:2-4). He did not object when Nicodemus said, "We know that thou are a teacher come from God: for no man can do these miracles that thou doest, except God be with him" (John 3:2). The blind man whom He healed believed on Him because of this miracle, and Christ took full advantage of that belief to press His claims to being the Messiah (John 9:35 f.). He refuted the Pharisees who had criticized Him for forgiving a man's sins, by pointing out that He was able to do the equally supernatural thing of instantly curing His sickness. "Whether is easier, to say, Thy sins be forgiven thee; or to say, Arise, and walk? But that ye may know that the Son of man hath power on earth to forgive sins, (then saith he to the sick of the palsy,) Arise, take up thy bed, and go unto thine house" (Matt. 9:5, 6).

The Messianic prophecies had frequently foreseen the

Messiah as a miracle worker. Jesus not only knew this but obviously pointed to Himself as qualified in this very particular. If He did not believe Himself to be possessed of supernatural powers, He must have known Himself to be engaged in palpable fraud and deliberate deception. So from the moral angle, if Christ wrought what He wrought merely by an unusual knowledge of nature and not by supernatural power, He must have been a lying deceiver. That is more difficult to believe than any miracle with which He has ever been credited.

Second, on the supposition before us, His own argument in His defense would be an argument against Him. That is to say, when the unbelieving Jews claimed that He did His works by the power of Beelzebub, He replied, "How can Satan cast out Satan? And if a kingdom be divided against itself, that kingdom cannot stand. And if a house be divided against itself, that house cannot stand. And if Satan rise up against himself, and be divided, he cannot stand, but hath an end" (Mark 3:23 ff.). But if Christ really did not do true miracles but only took advantage of His superior knowledge to play on the credulity of His times and later times, then He would have been perpetrating fraud as the prince of deceivers, and as such He would have been the devil's instrument. For He regarded the devil as the father of lies, and He would have been his son. Not only is such a thing utterly unthinkable from a moral standpoint, but it is, as His argument makes it, utterly irrational. For Satan would have been using lies to destroy his own kingdom. By these frauds of his servant Jesus, he would have been establishing the kingdom of Jesus which was founded on truth and which called men to repent of their sins. Thus Satan's house would have been divided against itself, for Christ, the son of lies, would by his lies have been destroying his father's kingdom of lies.

Third, if Christ had had the kind of knowledge which this

theory attributes to Him, such knowledge would have been as miraculous as the miracles it attempts to explain away. For centuries before and for centuries after, no other person but this solitary, untutored Jew knew how to walk on water. Modern science has performed many amazing feats in this century, but it still is nowhere nearer than it was in Jesus' day to multiplying loaves and fishes by a mere word. Machines can compare, classify, and do hitherto unbelievable things, but with all their powers they still depend on the feeble mind of man their inventor. They cannot even put a question to themselves but can only operate with their wonderful efficiency along channels made for them by men. Certainly none of them can anticipate an historical event tomorrow, much less predict the fall of a city a generation hence as precisely as Jesus did (Matt. 24:1 ff.). This explanation of the miracles of Jesus, therefore, requires as much, if not more, explanation than the miracles. It would be the miracle to end all miracles. Intellectually, it would be straining the gnat and swallowing the camel.

If the evidence is convincing that Christ did work miracles, what do these miracles prove? Miracles as such do not prove that Jesus was more than a man. For though men do not have this power as men, they could be enabled by God to perform them in His name. Miraculous power belongs only to the Author of nature, but it is apparently not incommunicable as God's omniscience, omnipotence, or eternality must be. So the power to work miracles is not necessarily proof that the person who has that power is God Himself. But it does prove him to be sent from God, for only God has this power and can delegate it. This is the very conclusion which Nicodemus drew when he said to Jesus, "We know that thou art a teacher come from God: for no man can do these miracles that thou doest, except God be with him" (John 3:2).

At this point, however, we face another problem or question. Is it not possible that there are other, nonhuman beings who, though not the Author of nature, are nevertheless able to influence nature in supernatural ways? Apart from revelation, we cannot know there are not such beings; we therefore consider the possibility that Christ's miracles were wrought by a man who had received His power from some supernatural being other than God, whether good or evil. If there are such beings and they are good, then they are in subjection to God and His servants. If, therefore, they communicated their powers to the man Jesus, they must have done so in obedience to the will of God. Thus their giving of power would be essentially the same thing as God's giving it, for they would give it in accordance with His will.

If these beings are evil beings, what then? Then they are not subservient to God and do not deliberately do His will. In that case they would not necessarily have power over nature, for that would obviously be in the hands of the Author of nature and of those to whom He willingly permits it to pass. If, therefore, these evil spirits possess any such power as we are here supposing, it can only be by the permission of God. So the question is, is it conceivable that God would permit these evil spirits to possess such power? Maybe we cannot answer that question, but we do not have to. The question that really concerns us here is not whether such spirits could possess such powers, but whether, even if they could, they would be able to communicate them to a human being. But we do not even have to answer that question, for we are dealing with a specific human being, Jesus Christ. So the question precisely is: if there are such evil beings and these beings are permitted by God to have power over nature which could conceivably be communicated to some human being, could they conceivably communicate it to such a human being as Jesus Christ? We have already shown that they could do so only if they wished to destroy themselves. They would be empowering Him to

make converts to a kingdom which was set up to destroy the
kingdom of evil. They would be giving power to one who
would use it only for good when, by definition, evil spirits
would want it to be used only for evil. They would be pro-
viding an instrument for healing when they wished only to
spread sickness and death; they would insure the success of
the person best fitted to insure their own failure. If these evil
spirits were intelligent spirits, they simply could not do such
a thing even if God would permit it. And is it possible that
God would communicate His great power to a man after His
own heart by spirits utterly alien to Him? So, from the standpoint of the devils themselves or from the standpoint of God
Himself, it would seem inconceivable that Christ's supernatural power could have been derived from Satan, if there
be such a being. And since there is no other conceivable
source from which His power could have come, it must have
come, as Nicodemus said, from God.

Supposing then that God does authenticate His own messengers by endowing them with miraculous powers but does
not thereby indicate that they are God, what do these miracles
prove about Jesus' divinity? They prove nothing directly,
everything indirectly. That is, the miracles as such do not
prove Jesus to be the Son of God; this power could have been
given to Him as a mere man. But indirectly they prove Him
to be the Son of God because they prove Him to be a truthful messenger, and this truthful messenger says that He is God.
Christ may have wrought miracles and not have been God;
but He could not have wrought miracles and said that He was
God without being God. The very miracles, as we have attempted to show, demonstrate Him to be an authenticated
messenger of God and require that all who respect God should
respect Him and hear His words. And His words, amazingly,
are that He himself is God. We are caught in a wonderful,
divine trap here. We cannot admit that Christ is a true miracle

worker without admitting that, in His case, His works prove His divinity. If it were not so, then we would have the impossible situation of thinking of God as accrediting a liar and sending a messenger with His own divine credentials to lead the world into delusion. This could not be. If miracles are what we have shown them to be and demonstrate what we have shown them to demonstrate, then they prove Jesus to have been who He says He is.

12

Prophecies of the Bible

A MORE extraordinary group of men has never appeared in history than the Old Testament prophets. They are equally noted for what has been called their "forthtelling" and their foretelling, their insight and their foresight. Their forthtelling, or their message to their contemporaries, carried its authority right on the surface. The very words carried an obvious imprimatur. On the other hand, their foretelling has waited for the ages to confirm, and the ages have surely done it.

Before we note how phenomenally their predictions were confirmed, it is well to observe a few preliminary matters. For one thing, it is remarkable that these men engaged in prediction at all. The history of religion affords few examples of it. For the most part, religious men restricted their deliverances concerning the future to very broad statements dealing with the general destiny of mankind. The Koran, for example, abounds in references to the coming hell and judgment, but Mohammedanism is conspicuously different in specifics from its Old Testament prophetic antecedents. Confucius is well known for having been preoccupied with this world; he abstained from even broad generalizatons about future destiny. Buddha was a philosopher whose predictions did not go much beyond the notion of a sphere of the realized ideal called nirvana. Students of history are the scholars least likely to prophecy the future, and the more learned the historian, the less likely is he to try. There are too many crucial contingencies—too many "ifs"—on which the wheels of history turn. They constrain the wise to say, "Boast not thyself of tomorrow for thou knowest not what the morrow will bring forth." But the Hebrew prophets predicted, with precise historical detail, things to come.

Perhaps the singularity of the Old Testament prophets will appear more clearly by contrast with others who did aspire to a certain degree of prediction. Thus Albert Barnes in *The Evidences of Christianity* mentions the case of the historian Macaulay, who made the following prediction concerning the future of the Roman Catholic Church: ". . . she may still exist in undiminished vigor when some traveler from New Zealand shall, in the midst of a vast solitude, take his stand on a broken arch of London Bridge to sketch the ruins of St. Paul's." W. F. Albright, in an address on the Old Testament prophets, compared them with Heinrich Heine and others who seemed to have an extraordinary sensitivity to the future. Another example of prophecy is found in the ancient oracles which were expected to give predictions and often did. One typical example is the answer which Maxentius received from the Sibylline books when he consulted them before his battle with Constantine at the Tiber River: "On that day the enemy of Rome will perish." The differences between these instances and Biblical prophecies are numerous.

The first difference between the Biblical prophets and others is that there was no "may" in the prophets' messages. Tentativeness is evident in Macaulay, for example, but there is ringing certainty in the prophets' predictions and not the hesitating speculativeness of the historian's guess.

Second, most of these extra-Scriptural writers lay no claim to divine enlightenment. That these men were capable of shrewd expectations or even of uncanny insight, no one wishes to contest. But not even they claimed anything more than that. The prophets, on the other hand, gave no evidence of being geniuses of occult insight but very frankly claimed God as the source of their information.

Third, in none of the cases of prediction that have been given or that could be given, do we find anything comparable to the degree of specificity found in the Biblical prophets' foretelling. To be sure, Macaulay was specific enough with his lonely New Zealander sitting on an arch of Westminster and painting the ruins of St. Paul's, but this was nothing more than the broadest of guesses, as he indicated. Furthermore, we have no fulfillment as yet, nor does anyone expect any. And the pagan oracles were notoriously "ambiguous, and with double sense deluding." Thus the words of the Sibylline to Maxentius carefully avoid defining the "enemy of Rome." Whoever perished would be the enemy of Rome, and the prediction would, by definition, be fulfilled. Maxentius may have comforted himself that Constantine was the enemy of Rome, but his own perishing proved him to be. This ambivalent type of prophecy could never be wrong; neither could it be right.

We will note a few of the innumerable predictions of the prophets, the remarkable fulfillments of which have confirmed their claims that they spoke the Word of the Lord. Then, we shall consider their most remarkable prediction of all, that of the advent of Christ. For convenience, we will arrange predictions and fulfillments in parallel columns so that the reader may more easily see the correspondence in detail.

TYRE

Prophecies	Fulfillment
1) "Thus saith the Lord God, I will bring upon Tyrus Nebuchadnezzar, king of Babylon, a king of kings, from the north, with horses and with chariots, and with horsemen ... He shall slay thy people by the sword, and thy strong garrisons shall go down to the ground" (Ezek. 26:7-11).	Nebuchadnezzar besieged the city of Tyre for thirteen years, according to the Jewish historian, Josephus, who cited the Greek historian, Menander.
2) "Pass ye over to Tarshish, howl ye inhabitants of the isle" (Is. 23:6). "The isles that are in the seas shall be troubled at thy departure" (Ezek. 26:18).	Tyrians later settled many colonies including Carthage and Tartessus in Spain
3) "And it shall come to pass in that day, that Tyre shall be forgotten for seventy years, according to the days of one king" (Is. 23:15-17; cf. Jer. 25:11, 12).	This was the duration of the Babylonian ascendancy.
4) "Howl ye inhabitants of the isle" (Is. 23:6). "What city is like Tyrus, like the destroyed in the midst of the sea?" (Ezek. 27:32).	Tyre moved to the island after the destruction of the mainland city by Nebuchadnezzar.
5) "And they shall lay thy stones and thy timber and thy dust in the midst of the waters" (Ezek. 26:12).	Alexander the Great built a half-mile causeway using the ruins of the old city and even scraping up the dust.

6) "I will bring forth a fire from the midst of thee . . . I will bring thee to ashes upon the earth in the sight of all them that behold thee" (Ezek. 28:18; cf. Zech. 8:1).

After besieging and taking the city, Alexander set it on fire (Quintus Curtius, *History of Alexander the Great,* Bk. 4, ch. 3). Eight thousand were killed, two thousand crucified and thirty thousand sold for slaves.

7) "I will make thee like the top of a rock, thou shalt be a place to spread nets upon; thou shalt be built no more" (Ezek. 26:14).

Not rebuilt to this day.

SIDON

"I will send into her pestilence and blood into her streets; and the wounded shall be judged in the midst of her, by the sword upon her on every side" (Ezek. 28:22, 23).

In 351 B.C., when the Sidonians rebelled against the Persians, their own king betrayed them and 40,000 shut themselves up in their houses to which they set fire. The city has been rebuilt and re-razed many times. It has about 15,-000 inhabitants today.

EGYPT

1) "Egypt . . . and . . . her cities shall be a desolation forty years . . . At the end of forty years will I gather the Egyptians from the peoples whither they were scattered; and I will bring back the captivity of Egypt, and will cause them to return . . . into the

Egypt was made captive and desolate under Nebuchadnezzar for forty years. It was later conquered by the Persians in 525 B.C. and made a vassal for a century. Alexander the Great subjugated it to the dynasty of Ptolemies. It has gradually been diminished until land of their habitation, and they shall be there a base kingdom. It shall be the basest of the kingdoms . . . and I will diminish them, that they shall no more rule over the nations" (Ezek. 29:12-15).

today it is a poverty-stricken nation.

2) "I will make the land waste, and all that is therein, by the hand of strangers . . . And there shall be no more a prince from the land of Egypt" (Ezek. 30:12, 13).

Egypt has had a king for most of the time since the prophecy, but none were native Egyptians. The country has been ruled by a series of foreigners: Persians, Greeks, Romans, Arabs, Turks, French and English.

3) "I will make the rivers dry" (Ezek. 30:12). "And the waters shall fail from the sea, and the river shall be wasted and dried up. And they shall turn the Rivers far away; the brooks of defence shall be emptied and dried up" (Is. 19:5, 6).

Originally about one-third of the nation's revenue was spent keeping canals clear. Since the Mohammedan conquest, the canals have been neglected. Even today canals do not serve nearly as much territory as formerly.

4) "The reeds and flags shall wither" (Is. 19:6).

Foliage has all but disappeared from the Nile.

5) "And the fishers shall mourn and all they that cast angle into the brooks shall lament, and they that spread nets upon the waters shall languish" (Is. 19:8).

Fish are few today and the industry unimportant.

We take one more instance of the predictive gift of the prophets before coming to the foretelling of the Christ. Next to Messianic prophecy, this one, which concerns the Jews, is the most astounding and therefore best-suited, not only to illustrate the prophetic gift, but to introduce us to our main point.

The most amazing thing about the Jews is that they have been dispersed from their own land for so long a time. What is yet more amazing is that Moses predicted their dispersal more than a thousand years before the final phase of it took place. "And ye shall be plucked from off the land whither thou goest to possess it. And the Lord shall scatter thee among all people, from the one end of the earth even unto the other" (Deut. 28:63, 64). But more amazing still is the fact that in spite of the dispersal, which has lasted more than twenty-five hundred years, the Israelitish nation has maintained its integrity among the peoples of the earth. And most amazing of all, this too—the remarkable preservation within the remarkable dispersal—was predicted. "And yet for all that, when they be in the land of their enemies, I will not cast them away, neither will I abhor them, to destroy them utterly, and to break my covenant with them" (Lev. 26:44). In addition to these comprehensive, sweeping prophecies concerning the Jews, there have been many smaller and more detailed ones, such as their being taken captive on one occasion for seventy years; their being permitted to return under Cyrus, King of Persia; their devouring their own children in periods of very terrible persecution and suffering; and innumerable others. All in all, it is not surprising that Moses said, "And thou shalt become an astonishment, a proverb, and a byword, among all nations whither the Lord shall lead thee" (Deut. 28:37); and that Frederick the Great received in answer to his demand, "Give me in one word, a proof of the truth of the Bible," the famous reply, "The Jews."

What did these mighty prophets of God have to say about their favorite theme, the coming Messiah? If they could foretell with matchless precision the downfall of the great but evil Babylon, we may well expect them to surpass themselves in foretelling the establishment of the Kingdom of God. If they could see Lucifer fallen from heaven, what could they see of the Son of God? If they amaze us with the wealth of detail with which these visitations of the divine wrath were to come upon the nations, what had they to say of the grace of God toward the world? We cannot help being filled with great expectations.

Old Testament prophecies of the Messiah are like the separate pieces of a jigsaw puzzle except that each separate part is intelligible in itself. Still, it is a part of a greater whole, not fully to be appreciated until set in its place in the greater whole. Thus, that a great personage is coming is shown by these statements collected by A. Alexander in his *Evidences of Christianity:* He should be "of 'the seed of the woman'; 'the seed of Abraham in whom all nations should be blessed'; 'the Shiloh who was to come out of Judah, before the dominion of that tribe should depart'; 'the prophet like unto Moses, whom the Lord would raise up'; 'the king whom the Lord would set upon his holy hill'; 'the priest after the order of Melchisedeck'; 'the anointed one, or Messiah'; 'the righteous branch'; 'the corner stone'; 'the desire of all nations'; 'the Shepherd of Israel.' " His forerunner is announced: "Behold, I will send my messenger, and he shall prepare the way before me: and the Lord whom ye seek, shall suddenly come to his temple, even the messenger of the covenant, whom ye delight in: behold, he shall come, saith the Lord of Hosts" (Mal. 3:1). The place of His birth is prophesied: "But thou, Bethlehem Ephratah, though thou be little among the thousands of Judah, yet out of thee shall he come forth unto me that is to be ruler in Irsael; whose goings forth have been from of old, from everlasting" (Micah 5:2). The nature of His work is foretold: "The Spirit of the Lord God is upon me; because the Lord hath anointed me to preach good tidings unto the meek; he hath sent me to bind up the broken-hearted, to proclaim liberty to the captives, and the opening of the prison to them that are bound; to proclaim the acceptable year of the Lord, and the day of vengeance of our God; to comfort all that mourn; to appoint unto them that mourn in Zion, to give unto them beauty for ashes, the oil of joy for mourning, the garment of praise for the spirit of heaviness; that they might be called trees of righteousness, the planting of the Lord, that he might be glorified" (Isa. 61:1-3). The Triumphal Entry was described by the prophet Zechariah (9:9): "Rejoice greatly, O daughter of Zion; shout, O daughter of Jerusalem: behold, thy King cometh unto thee: he is just, and having salvation; lowly, and riding upon an ass, and upon a colt the foal of an ass." The mysterious character of His person (divine and human) and ministry (lowly and exalted) are described centuries before. His humanity is shown in this prophecy cited immediately above and His divinity in the words of David (Ps. 110:1): "The Lord said unto my Lord, Sit thou at my right hand, until I make thine enemies thy footstool." In Isa. 53 we find a remarkable blend of the lowly and exalted: "He is despised and rejected of men; a man of sorrows, and acquainted with grief: and we hid as it were our faces from him; he was despised, and we esteemed him not. . . . Therefore will I divide him a portion with the great, and he shall divide the spoil with the strong; because he hath poured out his soul unto death: and he was numbered with the transgressors. . . ." Details of His death and burial are also indicated in this remarkable passage: "And he made his grave with the wicked, and with the rich in his death. . . ." Likewise His resurrection and ascension were foreseen: "For thou wilt not leave my soul in hell; neither wilt thou suffer thine Holy One to see corruption" (Ps. 16:10). Finally, His everlasting kingdom was a matter of prophecy: "I saw in the night visions, and, behold, one like the Son of man came with the clouds of heaven, and came to the Ancient of days, and they brought him near before him. And there was given him dominion, and glory, and a kingdom, that all people, nations, and languages, should serve him: his dominion is an ever-lasting dominion, which shall not pass away, and his kingdom that which shall not be destroyed" (Dan. 7:13, 14).

Canon Liddon has stated that there are in all more than three hundred prophecies in the Old Testament concerning the coming Messiah. All have been fulfilled, more or less fully and clearly, in Jesus of Nazareth. Someone has taken the trouble to calculate that the possibility of their being fulfilled in one person by sheer chance is one over 84,000,000,000,000,-000,000,000,000,000,000,000,000,000,000,000,000,000,000,-000,000,000,000,000,000,000,000,000,000,000,000,000,000,-000,000,000,000,000,000,000,000,000th of 1 per cent.

13

Archaeology of the Bible

NEITHER archaeology nor any other science can ever prove that the Bible is the inspired Word of God. But they could prove that it is not. Does this seem strange or unfair? It isn't really. The nature of the Bible makes it inevitable. The Bible claims to be inspired history. Its inspiration cannot be tested by archaeology, but obviously its history can be; at least some of its history can be. As Herman Ridderbos has well said, the Bible "is, if you please, *redemptive* history; but then, too, redemptive *history*." Archaeology, as such, cannot say whether the Bible has anything redeeming about it, but it knows whether there is anything historical about it. If the Bible were not a history book and if the Christian religion were not based on historical fact, then what the historical sciences have to say would be irrelevant so far as the Bible and the Christian religion are concerned. But since the Bible is, incidentally, a history book, and the Christian religion is a historically oriented religion, these sciences are relevant. To put the matter very bluntly, if it could be proved that Jesus Christ never lived, the Christian religion would immediately cease to be. If the Resurrection could be shown not to have taken place, then the salvation which is based on it would be an illusion. "And if Christ be not risen, then is our preaching vain, and your faith is also vain."

Yes, the Bible is a historical book, and it is willing to be subjected to any legitimate test of historical accuracy. No doubt the science most able to do that is the science of archaeology, and so we turn our attention to the verdict of this science about the historicity of the Christian faith. We do not expect it to be able to test every historical utterance in the entire Bible, but we are interested to hear what it has to say about those it has been able to test.

There is no doubt that Professor William Foxwell Albright, of Johns Hopkins University, is one of the greatest living archaeological authorities. He has been called "America's most distinguished scholar." The scope and the detail of his knowledge is a matter of amazement to any who are acquainted with his work. He has written many definitive books and made numerous important field studies, but for our purposes here the most convenient of his writings is his recent article on "archaeology" in the *New Schaff-Herzog Religious Encyclopedia*.[1] We shall rely mainly on this survey in our brief consideration of the subject, although Dr. Albright may not be held responsible for anything not in quotation marks.

There has, of course, been no "dig" of the Garden of Eden although the site has been generally agreed upon. About all that archaeology can do for the early chapters of Genesis is show whether they have the flavor of authenticity. "The stories of Genesis 1-11," says Dr. Albright, "are very ancient, and can in large part be traced eastward to the valleys of the Euphrates and Tigris. This is particularly true of the account of creation in Genesis 2:4 ff., of the story of Eden, of the lists

[1] L. A. Loetscher, ed.; used by kind permission of Baker Book House, Grand Rapids, Mich.

of antediluvian patriarchs, of the story of the Flood, and of the Tower of Babel."

Much research has gone into the patriarchal period which occupies the rest of the Genesis account (*ca.* 2000 to 1500 B.C. or the Middle Bronze Age). Many personal names appear and, moreover, "the Patriarchal customs are strikingly like the customs of northern Mesopotamia, as reflected in the Nuzi tablets of the fifteenth century B.C., which transmit practices inherited from earlier centuries."

The Exodus era has been especially well illuminated by the discoveries of archaeological studies. ". . . the names of Moses and other members of his family can be identified with Egyptian names popular at that time. There are also many indications of indirect Egyptian influence on Mosaic thought and life . . ." The Code of Hammurabi, the Sumerian Code of Lipit-Ishtar, and the Code of Eshnunna among some others "furnish us extraordinary insight into the background of the Book of the Covenant (Ex. 21-23) and other Mosaic jurisprudence."

The Conquest of Canaan is corroborated by two kinds of evidence. "Direct information on the Israelite occupation of Canaan comes from the Israel Stele of Pharaoh Marniptah (*ca.* 1223-16), where the Israelites appear as nomads who menace Egyptian control of Palestine and are duly punished. Indirect evidence comes, e.g., from the ruins of such important Canaanite towns as Lachish, Bethel, and Tell Beit Mirsim (Debir?), all destroyed by fire in the thirteenth century B.C. and reoccupied by bearers of a different and much cruder material culture. From the results of excavations we see that most of these destroyed towns were rebuilt almost immediately, but that towns such as Jericho were not rebuilt for centuries (cf. Josh. 6:20)."

Incidental light is thrown on the culture of the period of the First Monarchy. For example, "Glueck's excavation of the Solomonic seaport at Ezion-geber has brought to light copper refineries of a degree of development not hitherto considered possible in such an early period." Dr. Albright does not mention (nor is there any reason why he should) that many were the critics of the Bible who were accustomed to use the absence of positive proof for a Biblical statement as evidence that the statement was wrong. Such evidence as is now forthcoming supports the integrity of the Biblical witness, of course, but let it be said that it is also a reminder that the mere absence of confirmation is no argument against a statement.

Again, "until the discovery at Ugarit and decipherment of the long-lost Canaanite religious literature in the thirties of this century, it was impossible to present an objective argument for dating much Hebrew poetry before the ninth century B.C., in accord with Biblical tradition. Now the situation has changed drastically. A great many Hebrew poems employ poetic forms and stylistic devices characteristic of Canaanite poems composed before the fourteenth century B.C. . . . Moreover, the Psalter includes many archaic psalms (29, 68, etc.) which contain much phraseology of Canaanite origin and which must therefore go back to before the ninth century B.C. In particular we have many psalms which date back to about the tenth century and may easily reflect the taste of King David for music and poetry, as recorded by tradition."

The three centuries from the death of Solomon to the Fall of Jerusalem are now "very well illustrated by archaeology." Albright lists many of the findings inside and outside of Palestine which explain the history of these years.

"Our knowledge of the period from the fall of Jerusalem to the Macedonian conquest in 330 B.C. owes even more than that of the preceding period to archaeology. Excavation and surface examination of scores of sites of pre-exilic towns of Judah have proved conclusively that the Chaldean conquest was accompanied by a thorough-going devastation of the country, whose towns were not rebuilt for generations, if at all. There is no archaeological basis for the frequently expressed view that life continued in Judah during the Exile much as it had before—that there was no real break in Jewish life at this time. The traditional view is correct, though it must naturally be modified at points, where new information fills previous gaps in our knowledge."

Our knowledge of the New Testament is also greatly enriched by the archaeological research of the last century, and especially by the recent discovery of the Dead Sea Scrolls. Dr. Albright finds that these manuscripts bridge the gap between some intertestamental apocryphal books and the New Testament. John the Baptist "was certainly influenced by them, and we find their language and style strikingly similar to corresponding features of the Gospel of John, with echoes in the Synoptic Gospels and the Pauline Epistles." He concludes: "It is no longer possible to attribute the Gospel of John to a Gnostic writer; we have in these scrolls part of the pre-Gnostic background of thought and language in which Jesus grew up."

The great significance of this last fact, Albright does not feel it necessary to stress since he is not writing a book on Christian evidences but on archaeology. But by the same token, we will be excused here if we do point out the great significance for Christian truth in this discovery. For a century, very many Biblical critics opposed the traditional position which attributed the fourth Gospel to John. This was done in spite of strong external ecclesiastical evidence from early times that the apostle John was the author, as well as the claim of the book itself to have been written by an eye-witness. Johannine authorship was rejected with an amazing unanimity by liberal and radical scholars largely because the ideas in the Gospel were thought to be too advanced and theological for an apostle of the Nazarene. One has to read the books of these authors to realize how confident they were of their position, and how scornful of all who disagreed. For years whether a man believed in Johannine authorship or not was an unofficial test of scholarship. It is not exaggerating the matter to say that persons, however great their learning may have been, were scorned as naïve, simple-minded, and highly subjective because they could believe the traditional position. The ideas expressed in this Gospel had to come from the second century at the earliest. It was not thinkable that they should have come from the first century, from an eye-witness and apostle. We are not resenting past treatment, nor trying to take refined vengeance in the form of "I told you so," but merely warning again of the great danger of prejudging any matter and declaring something impossible simply because one cannot at the moment see how it could be possible.

It is well to observe here—and this includes a mild stricture of Albright himself—that because the presence of the Dead Sea Scrolls proves that it was possible for John to have had the ideas which he expressed in his Gospel, it by no means follows that it was because of the tradition represented by these Scrolls that he had the ideas he had. *Post hoc ergo propter hoc* ("after this therefore because of this") is no sounder a principle in Biblical criticism than it is anywhere else in the realm of logical thought. That the Essenelike group around the Dead Sea used language and ideas like John's proves indeed that such language and ideas did not have to come from a later period, but it does not prove that John's use of them came from this group. There may have been other groups whose writings we may not yet have found nor may ever find. On the other hand, since the language is essentially simple and only the thoughts are transcendent and sublime, it remains a possibility that John used this language and these ideas because they were all he knew which could fit the Christ of whom he wrote. Furthermore, what right have we to read into Johannine concepts any of the notions of the Dead Sea community simply because they preceded John in time? To sum the whole matter up, the Dead Sea Scrolls do not necessarily show the origin of John's language and ideas. They show simply that it is wrong to say that John could have derived them only from later groups such as the Gnostics since there were earlier Jewish examples at hand. Independently of whether the Dead Sea Scrolls had been found or not, it remains true that one cannot say of a writer that he could have expressed himself in a particular manner of thought only if he had earlier copies before him.

"Turning to Palestinian archaeology in the narrow sense, many buildings of this age have been excavated. The excavations in Jerusalem have brought to light extensive remains of Herodian and early Roman times in the Temple area, especially the exterior of the retaining wall of the Herodian temple enclosure and the substructure and pavement of the Praetorium at the Tower of Antonia. The line of the First and Second Walls of Herod has been traced in large part, and the long-lost line of Agrippa's wall is now known. . . ."

Albright concludes the survey with these words: "Without archaeology it thus becomes impossible really to understand New Testament history." If he will substitute the word "fully" for "really," we will gladly concur in the judgment. But we note here especially that not only does archaeology help us to understand the Biblical story; it also helps us to believe it. That is to say, in very many instances what men have thought was not and could not be true, archaeology has shown could be and was true. Incident after incident, custom after custom, narrative after narrative have been substantiated by the spade. The Bible has not only "come alive," but it has come with a new ring of historical authenticity. The stones

have indeed cried out their hosannahs. As another archaeological expert, Millar Burrows of Yale University, has said,
"On the whole . . . archaeological work has unquestionably
strengthened confidence in the reliability of the Scriptural
record. More than one archaeologist has found his respect for
the Bible increased by the experience of excavation in Palestine."

When we put together something of the picture, science
appears as a true handmaid of religion, a tutor to lead to
Christ. The Garden no longer sounds to men like mere myth-
ology, nor the Flood so impossible. Abraham has become
a man and not merely a name. Chedorlaomer comes alive,
and his route is put on the map. Sodom and Gomorrah have
been dug out of their brimstone. Moses has learned to write,
and the things he wrote were not so remote from his times
as men thought. The sojourn of Israel in Egypt receives historical confirmation, and her exodus is dated. The journey
through the wilderness is no longer so trackless. The walls of
Jericho have fallen inward in our times, and Joshua's conquest
no longer seems farfetched. David's kingdom is filled out, and
the Queen of Sheba seems, not legendary, but real. Job has
regained his antiquity. Mosaic monotheism is not just special
pleading any more. We have found the stalls of Solomon's
horses and the temple David built. Archaeologists have dug
Hezekiah's viaduct, and men are no longer so sure that Daniel
was much later than tradition has it. Cyrenius could have
been governor, as the third Gospel says, when the census was
made which brought the infant Jesus to Bethlehem. Herod
the Great is now an open book. Luke's reputation as an historian has been restored and enhanced by the studies of
Ramsey and others on the book of the Acts, and, one by one,
Paul's epistles have been given back to him. And so gradually,
day by day and year by year, the researches of men have

tended to vindicate the historical accuracy of the Word of God.

As we said at the beginning of this chapter, we do not expect anyone to become a believer in the inspiration of the Scripture because of the work of the archaeologists. But on the other hand, we do not think that men can help gaining a greater respect for the historical integrity of the Bible from their work. Certainly one cannot well become an unbeliever on the basis of the spade. Rather we suppose that, respecting the basic reliability of the Bible, one may well be disposed to consider its claim for its own inspiration, which argument we have tried to set forth.

14

The Biblical Religion

WE HAVE presented evidence intended to show that the Bible is the revelation of God. It is time now to outline in a more systematic manner what the Bible teaches. The statements of doctrine that follow are drawn from the Bible, although it has not seemed necessary to give the numerous texts which could be adduced in their support.

First, Scripture presents the very God whom nature required to explain all that is. He is an independent, eternal, omniscient, moral being. He is the author and governor of all that is. This God is a personal being as we were led to expect, and His fundamental attribute is the very holiness which is reflected in the constitution of man. Furthermore, God is a tripersonal being in one essence—a Trinity. This was not intimated in nature unless the revelation that God is good and loving led us to suppose that there must be more persons than one in the Godhead to participate in this eternal love.

Man's creation and fall neatly fit what a rational mind could have anticipated. Man is a creature of this First Cause of all being. That he was created in the very image of God explains the moral consciousness with which we are all familiar. We have noticed, to use the expression of Kant, that we have a "categorical imperative," or built-in moral law, and that this argues the existence of a lawgiver. Scripture tells us that the moral governor of the universe made us with the capacity for ethical discrimination and, on the basis of it, holds us morally responsible. It is the mind of man which makes him superior to the animals though they excel him greatly in physical strength. Likewise, we learn from the Bible that even man's scientific research into the nature of things was an assignment given to him by God from the very beginning of his creation.

The Bible tells how sin came into the world. Otherwise, we would wonder how God, who is manifestly good, could be the author of such confusion and darkness and evil. The Bible answers the question. He was not the author of evil. At the same time, nothing came into being without His will. The Bible explains that He created man good and in His own image. As a free moral agent, man was able to do evil and God permitted him to do it. God did not tempt him to evil; He rather warned him solemnly against it. But neither did He render him incapable of it.

We wonder how a being that was good and had no inclinations toward evil could ever be tempted. What was there in him to which solicitation could be addressed? Only the virtues with which his Maker had endowed him, says the Bible. That is, the eyes by which he saw the tree of temptation were God's good gift to him; it was not sinful for him to appreciate beauty. God also gave him the understanding by which he recognized that the fruit could make one wise; it was not sinful to desire wisdom. Rather, the temptation was directed to the misuse of legitimate propensities—misuse, because God had previously forbidden that they should be indulged in this case. No new principle was at work in causing man to yield, but only his God-given faculties. The sin lay in disregarding the commandment of God.

The Bible also explains how this single sin, once committed by one man, became a corruption in the heart of the entire human race. We are all now aware that "to err is human." Evil is so universal that it has become somehow associated with the very heart of every man. That every person should grow up and do evil can be no coincidence. It calls for an explanation. The Bible gives the explanation. The nature of mankind became corrupt by the transgression of the first parent of mankind. Reflection reveals that this is indeed the only tenable explanation of what has become a recgonized fact: universal sin.

It also seems manifestly rational that the race should have been tried by the behavior of the first parent. It was the only way that a race such as the human race could have been morally tested. The angels were tested individually, some succeeding and some failing in their probation and each being judged accordingly. Angels are represented as sexless beings who are not married and do not live in families. Since man is not such a creature but does reproduce and live in families in which the progenitors influence their offspring, he could not have been fairly tested individually. Every individual influences another, so the ideal situation could be preserved only for one person. The Bible, therefore, represents God as creating the first man perfect, and placing him in ideal circumstances, and giving him the greatest possible incentives to do good. Indeed, these incentives were greater for him than they could have been for any other individual since it was apparently made clear that the fate of the whole race depended on him. If persons had been tried individually, the incentive of concern for the whole human race would not have been present as it was when the race was tried by a single representative.

The fall of man accounts not only for spiritual death but for physical death as well. We have become used to mortality since that is all we have ever known. Still, mortality is not natural to man, is it? Death is the result of decay and decadence, a blight on life. There is nothing in nature as such which explains why a creature made in the image of the immortal God should be naturally subject to decay and death. Such a condition is unnatural on the surface of it. Only some catastrophe could have brought man into this condition. And the catastrophe must have been moral in character since it brought the displeasure of the moral First Cause (for what could make nature unnatural but the Cause of nature?) into such awful expression. Sin, or moral aberration, does not come about because men are mortal, born with the seeds of death and decay in them. It must have been conceived at the beginning of the human race by someone who represented us all. In other words, the Bible confirms the suggestions of nature, telling us that the man's name was Adam and describing the character of his trial and the sin and the consequences, with which we are all too familiar.

Redemption is the central theme of the Scripture. According to the Bible, man after his fall deserved to perish, for "the wages of sin is death." But men did not immediately perish because "where sin abounded, grace did yet more abound." From Gen. 3:15 on, the Old Testament is concerned with announcements of and preparations for the coming of the Saviour into the world. When the Christ is about to be born, His name is to be called Jesus, for "he shall save his people from their sins."

Jesus Christ, the God-man, was perfectly suited to be the Saviour of the fallen human race. As a Man He was able to identify Himself with men; as God He was able to make an infinite satisfaction for sins. If He had been merely man, His atonement could have had only finite value. Had He been merely God, He could not have been tempted, nor could He have died to make satisfaction. But in His two natures He was able to perform the duties incumbent on men while possessing the prerogatives which belong only to divinity.

His actual work of redemption is called in the Bible justification. Justification has been classically defined as "a work of God's free grace wherein he pardoneth our sins and accepteth us as righteous in his sight only for the righteousness of Christ imputed to us and received by faith alone." It has two parts, remission and righteousness. By the work of remission, Christ as the Mediator receives the punishment due to sinners. He interposes His precious blood for them. He is beaten with their stripes. He who knew no sin becomes sin that they might become the righteousness of God in Him. He came, he said, to minister and to give His life a ransom for many. In Him all died. These are various and sundry ways by which the Bible expresses the doctrine that Christ in His humanity received the judgment of God upon sin, with which He was vicariously identified. He likened Himself to the serpent (usually the symbol of sin in the Bible) lifted up in the wilderness (referring to His death on the cross), where He was so identified with the sin of His people that the Father in anger hid His face from Him. Christ abandoned and alone, forsaken of God, cried out, "My God, my God, why hast thou forsaken me?" Thus He "was delivered up for our offenses."

According to the Bible, man was originally created holy, right, and good, but not immutably so. Subsequently, he lost the goodness he had. So the work of redemption, if it was to be more perfect than the original righteousness of man, had to restore that original righteousness and do more. The "more" which it had to do was to make that original righteousness permanent and inalienable. This Christ has done for His people in what is called "justification" proper. He makes them righteous. They are not only freed from guilt by the remission of sins, but they are endowed with positive righteousness. Thus they are rendered more than "not guilty"; they are made "accepted in the Beloved." For he "who was delivered up for our offenses, was raised again for our justification." Consequently, "who shall lay anything to the charge of God's elect?" It is Christ Jesus who died, yea rather, that rose again."

But while Christ restores the image of God, reconciles believers to God through His new and living way, and makes them acceptable in His sight, He does not utterly remove remaining sin. He washes the body, but He does not make it impossible for Christians to get their feet dirty in their journey through this world (John 13:1 ff.). He grafts them into Himself as branches in a vine, but not in such a way that they do not need further and constant pruning by the divine Husbandman (John 15:1 ff.). His greatest disciple could say, "I am crucified with Christ: nevertheless I live; yet not I, but Christ liveth in me: and the life that I now live in the flesh I live by the faith of the Son of God, who loved me, and gave himself for me." On the other hand he could say, "I count not myself to have attained," and "I press on for the mark of the prize of the high calling of God in Christ Jesus." The apostle John, whom Christ loved especially, said, "He that saith he hath no sin deceiveth himself and the truth is not in him."

But the Second Adam was to secure a salvation for His people which the First Adam was not able to secure for those whom he represented. While the latter lost what was potentially theirs, Christ gained actual salvation for them. He made it impossible for them ever to fall again. "No one," he said, "shall take them out of my hand." "The Lord knows his own," and therefore the "foundation of the Lord stands sure," echoed the apostle Paul. "He who hath begun a good work

in you will continue it to the day of Christ." Jesus Himself
even defined discipleship in terms of persevering: "If ye continue in my word, then are ye my disciples indeed." Thus,
one who perseveres is a disciple; one who does not persevere
is not (never was) a disciple.

Such is the wisdom of God, however, that the Christian is
given ultimate assurance of his redemption in such a way
that his assurance in no way contributes to carnal presumption
or moral indifference. Thus Christ, who assured His disciples
that no one would take them out of His hand, also commanded them to abide in Him lest they be cut off as dead
branches (John 15:1 ff.). Similarly, the apostle Paul, while
certain that He who had begun a good work would continue
it, beat his own body lest while he preached to others he
should himself be a "castaway" (I Cor. 9:27). There is no
inconsistency or paradox in such statements. They merely
bring out two aspects of the same truth: on the one hand,
perseverance is a divine certainty, and on the other, perseverance is by means of human effort. Persevering persons
will persevere, that is, continue living holily. Those who do
not continue living holily are not even disciples. Scripture
does not say that the Christian may cease to be a Christian. It
says merely that if a professed Christian does not abide in
Christ and bear fruit, he is not a Christian; he shall be cast
off like a dead branch. Paul, to be sure, says that if he should
cease to beat his body, he would be a castaway. He does not
say that he ever will cease to beat his body. On another occasion he said that if an angel should ever preach any gospel
other than the true one, the angel would be anathema. He
does not say that an angel ever would so preach. Jesus Christ
Himself says that if He spoke as the Pharisees, He would be
a liar too; but He does not say, or infer, that He was capable
of ever so speaking. Thus judiciously does the plan of salvation insure at once confidence and humility in the believer.

He is assured that God is working in him to will and to do according to His good pleasure, and at the same time he is to work out his own salvation with fear and trembling.

This is probably the proper place at which to mention God's plan of redemption. First of all, God must be omniscient, must He not? We have already shown that He is independent, and all other things are dependent on Him. That implies that nothing can ever come into being but by His will. And since He must eternally know His own will, He must be omniscient. Since God is omniscient, He must know all things pertaining to salvation and men's responses to it. He must, in other words, know who will and who will not believe, persevere, and be saved. But if He does know all these things in advance of their eventuating, then He must be absolutely certain in advance of their occurrence. If they are not certain, they cannot be known as certain. God cannot know a lie; that is, He cannot know something as certain which is actually uncertain. But if God does know things, even the salvation of men, as certain beforehand, then they must be certain beforehand. But what could make them certain in advance? Nothing but God Himself, obviously. Therefore, God must decree them to come to pass or predestinate the actions of men. At the same time, He must do so consistently with human freedom, for man is free and his actions are unforced. He is a responsible moral agent.

The Bible does present both of these lines of teaching. A large number of passages show the sovereignty of God in the affairs of men (Is. 44:28; 46:10; Eph. 1:5; Lam. 3:37; Matt. 11:25 f.; Acts 2:23,28). A large number of texts indicate the freedom and responsibility of men (Matt. 17:12; Acts 2:23; Ezek. 18:2 f.; Rev. 3:20; John 7:17; Luke 9:23). The Bible sees and feels no contradiction between these two conceptions, nor has any man ever shown that there is any. Mystery, yes; contradiction, no.

As the Bible begins with God in eternity, so it ends with God and His creation in eternity. There is, said Augustine, just enough judgment in this world to show that there will be a judgment in the next world, but not enough in this world to make the judgment in the next world unnecessary. It was John Stuart Mill who observed that this world was in no sense ideal except as a place of probation. For that purpose it is perfectly suited. And so the Bible confirms. This is the day of probation, the time when men's destinies are worked out. "It is appointed unto men once to die, but after this the judgment." This judgment at death will be immediate, personal, and private. Man will in the intermediate state remain disembodied but in his place of final destiny, he will be in misery (Luke 16:20 ff.), or he will be blessed in Christ (Phil. 1.21 f.). The saints wait to be clothed upon (II Cor. 5:1 ff.), while the devils and, no doubt, lost men also, live in fear of the "resurrection" to death, the second death (Matt. 8:29). The Day of Judgment will be universal, visible, and public. All the hidden things will be brought to light, hidden wickedness and hidden faith and love. The Searcher of hearts will then make plain the hearts of men and the basis of His own judgment. Those who are wicked, whatever their outward appearances may have been, will be dismissed with the devil and his angels into eternal torment. Those who have been humble lovers and servants of God and their fellow men will thereby have exhibited the genuineness of their faith in Christ, by whom they are saved, and inherit the kingdom prepared for them before the foundation of the world. And so eternity will go on, hell with its miseries unending, total, unalleviated, hopeless; heaven with blessedness unending, perfect, undiminished, full of glory.

15

Some Doctrinal Difficulties in the Biblical Religion

UNDOUBTEDLY our brief sketch of the message of the Bible has raised various questions. This chapter is given over to a consideration of some of the principal queries and criticisms of Biblical teaching.

First, there is the question concerning the origin of sin. This problem is not peculiar to Christian theology. It confronts any theistic theology. If God is good and the author of all things, whence comes evil? If God is the author only of the good, who is the author of the evil? Since the good God is Himself the only ultimate author of all things, how could sin possibly originate at all?

This is the most difficult problem in all of theistic theology and philosophy. We suspect it is fundamentally unanswerable. Let us suppose for the moment that it is unanswerable. What then? Do we deny evil as Christian Science does? Or do we deny God as atheism and pantheism do? Either of these alternatives would be impossible. Why? Because the evidence for the existence of evil and the evidence for the existence of

God are irrefutable. Both clearly exist. The facts cannot be denied. Much of this book is written to prove the existence of God. Books hardly need to be written to prove the existence of sin. We can only declare that sin exists, God exists, and God is the ultimate cause of all things. He cannot be the immediate cause of sin since He is altogether good. He must, therefore, have brought evil about indirectly. How or why He did this we may not know. That He could and did do it the facts require. We must simply leave the matter there. This is what we call a mystery. We do not know how certain things have come to pass. We know only that they have come to pass.

In spite of what has been said, we do not suggest that no light at all can be shed on this great difficulty. First, we have already indicated that the original sin did not presuppose a sinful propensity. The things which tempted were not unnatural but natural, and man in yielding to them did not display the presence of an evil tendency, but the working of otherwise legitimate inclinations. The sin lay in wrongly using them, in disobedience to the command of God. Second, it may be observed, as Augustine and many others have shown, that sin or evil is not a positive principle but a negative one. That is, it is not a being or entity as God or the Good is; evil is the absence of God or the Good. It is not an efficient cause (*causa efficiens*), but a deficient cause (*causa deficiens*). It is not being, but a parasite of being. It cannot exist independently, but must be a falling away from true being. It is nevertheless real, although not ultimately real as true being or Good is. Third, a finite being may misjudge the infinite and thereby sin. The finite does not need to misjudge the infinite, but it may do so. Adam was able to sin, but he was also able not to sin.

In any case, an inability to explicate or comprehend does not constitute an objection to anything. While explication and proof may establish something, the inability to submit such proof does not disprove anything. That is, if there is evidence that a thing is so, the inability to explain how it is so cannot properly be considered an argument against the truth of it. For example, it is a mystery that this cold type on a dead page can communicate real meaning from a living author to a living reader. We know some of the steps of the process, but who is so rash as to say that he fully understands how intellectual concepts are conveyed by such material means? Or who is so rash as to doubt it?

A second query about the Christian faith concerns the doctrine of representation. Is it fair, the question is asked, for one man to be judged on the performance of another? May Adam, whom I never knew, stand or fall for me? Especially, may he fall and pull me down to hell with him? Is it right that my eternal destiny should rest on anyone but myself alone? Does every person not stand or fall by himself alone? Does the Bible itself not say that, "when the righteous turneth from his righteousness, and committeth iniquity, he shall even die thereby. But if the wicked turn from his wickedness, and do that which is lawful and right, he shall live thereby" (Ezek. 33:18,19)? Were the Israelites not rebuked for thinking that the fathers had eaten sour grapes and the children's teeth were set on edge? Is my son condemned for my sins? In other words, is trial by proxy true either to justice, life, or Scripture itself?

This point is, we believe, capable of a satisfactory rational answer. The objections we find to be more emotional than rational. We therefore ask the reader to consider this reply objectively, considering whether it answers the objection, not whether it appeals to his personal preference.

There are a number of considerations which justify the procedure indicated in the Bible. First, it should be remembered that the Judge of all the earth cannot do wrong (Gen.

18:25). If He has settled on such a method of probation, we may be sure that the method is consistent with the rules of justice which are nothing but an expression of His own just nature. Second, the nature of man requires such a probation rather than a trial by individuals, as we observed in the preceding chapter. If the first man, having been privately tried, had sinned and fallen, he might have fallen as one man only. But in his fallen condition he would have reproduced. and his children would have had corrupted natures and a corrupt environment in which to undergo their own probation. This surely would not be fair. Third, the circumstances of the Edenic probation were most ideal, and indeed better than they could have been for any other individual. Not only was the environment perfect and utterly conducive to obedience; not only were the dangers of disobedience sufficiently great and the advantages of obedience sufficiently wonderful; but all these favorable circumstances were made still more favorable by the fact that the probation was being undergone as a public and not as a private responsibility. That is, Adam no doubt was made to understand that the destiny of all his progeny would be determined by his behavior, which must have added incalculably to his motives for obedience. Thus he as an individual would be under more favorable circumstances than any other individuals could have been, even if they had not been corrupted by the bad example of predecessors. Fourth, there is analogy to this in life as we know it. There is a representative principle written large in the necessary affairs of men. Whatever form of government there be among men, it must necessarily be to some degree representative. One or few must act for the many, and the many must suffer or benefit from their decisions. This begins in the family in which the parents necessarily make many decisions for the children, and the children necessarily reap the consequences, good or ill. It could not be otherwise in the human family. It is true not only of the family but of church and of state, of small groups and of great. Fifth, the atonement rests squarely on the principle of representation. If it was possible for Christ to give His life a ransom for many, the principle of representation is established at the most important point in human destiny.

That God should be capable of vengeance and wrath is thought by some to be a concept unworthy of the Deity of whom the Scriptures teach. He would have to be a petty being, they say, unhappy until He gets even with His creatures. Vengeance is thought to be incompatible with the view of God as magnanimous and noble-minded and would present him as some small, vindictive, spiteful tyrant. To this we reply that the God of the Bible is an eternally glorious being, the only ultimately good and worthy and excellent sovereign of heaven and earth. If it is important for men to maintain the dignity of men, to respect those in authority, to honor father and mother, to rise up before the hoary head, to fear the king; it is infinitely more important for God to maintain the dignity of the Godhead. If we cannot permit men to cast aspersions on our parents or anyone else whom we respect, it is inconceivably greater evil to dishonor the majesty of heaven. If we are aware of this, God must be infinitely more aware of it. Suitable punishment for infraction of the honor of God is proper and necessary, inasmuch as the absence of it would be a tacit abnegation on the part of God of the glory and majesty of His person, and that would be unthinkable. In other words, punishment for sin, far from being a petty action, is an essential of infinite majesty. It is precisely because God is great and not small that He must maintain the glory of His name.

That Scripture itself opposes the vengeance of God is usually deduced from the Bible's representation of the divine being as infinitely good and merciful. This the Bible frequently does teach. Mercy is a distinguishing attribute of the God of the Scriptures. "God is love." There are, however, many other attributes of God as well. The Bible records these various attributes without separating them. It is precisely because men disregard the love of God and presume upon His mercy that God's glory and majesty call for suitable reprisal. It is a great sin to dishonor the mercy and love of God. No sin can be committed with impunity, certainly not a sin so heinous and odious as despising the very love which offers the forgiveness of sin. Psalm 95 begins with a most cordial invitation to come and worship God; it closes contemplating those who harden their hearts and warns them that God will swear in His wrath that they shall not enter into His rest. "How," asks the New Testament, "can we escape if we neglect so great salvation?" Jesus said that it would be more tolerable for Sodom and Gomorrah than for Chorazin and Bethsaida in the day of judgment, because these cities of Galilee had spurned so much more of the goodness and mercy of God than even the perverse Sodomites. If God's love and mercy were exposed to the despising of men, they could then turn and despise all His other attributes because they could presume on His mercy. They would utterly subvert the whole moral order, making God the slave of men, putting a premium on vice, turning hell into heaven and heaven into hell. In other words, if men could presume on the mercy of God, God would be at the mercy of men, rather than men at the mercy of God.

One of the great questions often asked of Christianity is how its teaching that God is sovereign and brings His will to pass can be reconciled with its equally emphatic teaching that men are free and responsible and that their actions determine their destiny. We will discuss this matter more fundamentally in the chapter dealing with determinism as an objection against the Christian faith. Let us simply say here in passing

that the Bible assumes each of these teachings to be true
and that they need no reconciliation because they are not
in conflict one with the other. Many persons do think that
there is some conflict between them, but they do not demonstrate it. It is often tacitly assumed that God cannot be
sovereign and man free. Seldom does it seem that anyone feels
it necessary to attempt to show why this must be so. Yet it is
by no means self-evident that it is impossible for God to
bring His will to pass in free agents without violating their
freedom. Or to put the matter another way, what proof is
there that it cannot be my will that I should type these words
and be God's will at the same time? The convergence or
confluence or coaction of two wills in the same thing without
coercion does not, on the surface of it, seem impossible. Of
course, if I did not will to type and some invisible force
constrained me to write against my will, that would be quite
a different matter. But I know that there is no external con-
straint forcing me to type. I am typing of my own volition.
But if someone tells me that in so doing I am carrying out
the eternal will of God, I will have no difficulty believing him
if he gives me some evidence that such is indeed the case.

Do we not manufacture this problem by assuming that
coaction necessarily means coercion? If this were necessarily
so, then there would indeed be a problem. But until it is
proved to be so, we can hardly admit that there is a problem
here. That the matter is mysterious, as we have said elsewhere,
no one can deny. That it is contradictory, paradoxical, or
conflicting, no one can affirm.

Probably the greatest objection which is ever raised against
the Christian faith is the perennial protest against eternal
punishment. Granted, some say, that sin must be punished.
Granted that God must avenge His honor and maintain His
majesty. Granted that He cannot permit His creatures to

despise their Creator. Still, why must the punishment be incredibly severe? Especially, why must it be endless? Is it right that a man should sin, however wickedly, persistently, and intentionally, and then be punished so terribly that one moment in hell brings more anguish than a century of the greatest tortures this world knows? Is it right that a man should sin for a time, perhaps even a hundred years, and afterward suffer unspeakably for all eternity without a moment's relief? Surely that cannot be mercy. But is it even justice?

Scripture does reveal this transcendently awful fact. Indeed it intimates that no man can actually conceive how terrible hell really is. "Who can know the power of his anger?" Let us, therefore, consider the reason for this admittedly dreadful retribution.

First, sin is committed against an infinite being. Manifestly, when we enrage an infinite being we stir up an infinite anger. If His love is infinite and if acceptance of it would bring eternal life, His love when spurned must bring infinite retribution. God is an infinite being, and He necessarily acts in an infinite mode. Second, hell is no more than sin deserves. The more obligation a man has to do anything, the more blame and retribution he incurs by not doing it. Thus, doing evil to one's mother is more heinous than doing evil to a stranger because one has more obligation to one's mother than to a stranger. But if a person has more obligation to love his mother than a stranger, he has infinitely more obligation to love God than to love his own mother. And if it is more reprehensible to do ill to one's mother than to a stranger, it is infinitely more reprehensible to do ill to God than to one's mother. Third, let us notice what happens when punishment is administered. When wicked men are punished, they resent it rather than welcome it, for they retaliate rather than repent; they are hardened rather than softened. Conse-

quently, they must be punished for the sin of resenting punishment, and the cycle necessarily goes on for all eternity
as long as the nature of man remains as it is. And God will
surely preserve man's nature as long as He needs to punish
it.

16

The Biblical Religion Compared with
Other Religions

LET US now, having considered Christianity in itself, compare it with the other principal religions of the world. As we have outlined the doctrines of the Christian faith in a preceding chapter, it may be well to examine these other religions with respect to some of the same teachings.

First, then, how do the religions of the world conceive of the Divine Being? Does the God they present correspond to the God revealed in the visible universe—a personal, intelligent, moral first cause? No, this God is actually found only in those religions of the world which derive from the Bible. That is to say, the only truly monotheistic religions are those whose monotheism has come from the special revelation of Scripture. These religions are Judaism, Christianity, and Islam. Hinduism is grossly polytheistic, and the philosophical form of it expressed in the Upanishads and Vedanta is pantheistic. Buddhism, which represents a reform in Hinduism, takes an atheistic position. A still later reform, Sikhism, is monotheistic, apparently because of its contact with Islam and Christianity. Confucianism, while it pays nominal adherence to traditional Chinese polytheism and ancestor worship, may be basically agnostic. Shinto is polytheistic. Thus, of the major religions of the world none has maintained a sound view of God except those which have derived that view directly or indirectly from the special revelation of the Bible.

What, secondly, of the doctrine of man found in these religions? It is obvious that if there be no personal God there can be no doctrine of creation. Nor can there be any notion of the unity of man if it is not based on a belief in a common Creator. Polytheism has made the caste system of Hinduism and Shintoism theologically possible. Buddhism has not been able to prevent a derogatory estimate of womankind because of its absence of a sound theism. Islam and Judaism hold a doctrine of man resembling that of Christianity because they are derived from the Bible. Their differentiation from Christianity does not yet appear manifestly.

How did sin come into the world and what is its nature, according to the religions of the world? Judaism has the Old Testament with its primary account (Gen. 3) of the origin of sin but without the profound interpretation of Paul in Rom. 5:12-21. To Judaism, Genesis is merely the example of a couple committing sin. Tradition has tended to replace Scripture as the significant criterion in relation to which sin is defined, the deficiency of which is that tradition is the word of man rather than the Word of God. Generally, Judaism holds a superficial view of sin, thinking only of outward transgressions and not inward corruption.

With Christianity, Islam agrees that Adam was the first sinner, that his and others' sins are defined in relation to the will of God, and that sin brings divine judgment now and hereafter. Apart from these resemblances, the Muslim doctrine is radically different. In the first place, the criterion of virtue, God's will, is arbitrary. Second, God Himself wills sin in an unqualified sense of that word, so that the man who sins is not a free moral agent. Furthermore, the first man who sinned did not undergo a corruption of his nature nor did his descendants. The race therefore follows Adam in sin merely by imitation. Finally, the wages of sin is not death, for God may without expiation forgive sin, and indeed man's destiny rests on the will of God irrespective of demerit.

For Hinduism, in the last analysis, sin has no real meaning. The gods commit certain evil deeds and are praised for them. Man, on the other hand, is liable to rebirth for good or evil deeds. Since rebirth itself is the misfortune, irrespective of the resultant condition, sin seems essentially the same as virtue. The ideal appears to be, not the absence of evil deeds, but the absence of any deeds (nirvana). The Hindu notion of sin is present in Buddhism in a more developed form. All desire is evil precisely because it necessitates rebirth. Not evil desires alone, but desire as such is sin. Gautama did prescribe certain do's and don't's, but these were only relative virtues and vices by which one was in a more or less favorable position to free himself from desire. In Sikhism also, we have the same basic conception of *Karma,* approximately, the laws of retribution and transmigration of souls after death into another form of existence with their implicit notion of sin. Confucianism thinks of man as by nature good. By attending to the moral law he may stay so. Education leads him to know and respect the moral law. Some Confucian thinkers take the notion of sin very seriously, but the prevailing doctrine has always been otherwise. Taoism is very little concerned with ethics and therefore has no sharp notion of sin. In the earlier phases of Shintoism there appears to have been a sin-conciousness comparable to that in primitive religion. But in modern times, right and wrong are defined in relation to the will of the Emperor. We look in vain, therefore, to the religions of the world for any adequate account of the nature and origin of the mystery of iniquity.

The most vital element in any religion is its plan of salvation. Modern Judaism, in spite of the elaborate exhibition in the Old Testament of the principle that "without the shedding of blood there is no remission of sin," is devoid of a doctrine of substitutionary atonement. A man must save himself. Jewish theology is as bloodless as the modern observance of the Passover. In Islam, sin is arbitrarily defined and as arbitrarily canceled. God may do so without satisfying the justice and holiness of His being; indeed He may forgive without the sinner's repentance. Islam is insistent that there can be no vicarious atonement. Alms and the like atone for sins.

Hinduism has a doctrine of salvation or deliverance from consciousness, rather than of sin. Deliverance takes place when the soul comes to recognize, not achieve, its unity with the All. Two standard schemes of salvation are in practice. First, the Hindu may be saved by faith (*bhakti*) in one of the more theistic deities (especially Ram and Krishnu). Second, he may be saved by the knowledge that he is one with the All and that all else is illusion. In Hinduism man continues to exist as a part of the All into which he is absorbed, but in Buddhism he loses all self-existence in the process of absorption. All desire must cease, therefore the desirer must cease. This ideal of no-life is achieved by the individual alone as he lives the good life. Mahayana Buddhism, especially in Tibet, has developed a more theistic mode of salvation. Sikhism teaches salvation by purgatorial transmigrations, and (showing its syncretistic character) by a way of devotion in reliance on the mercy of God. Confucius had no doctrine of salvation. Some Confucianists who have felt the lack have accepted the way of *bhakti* of the Amita Buddha. Taoism teaches transmigration as a two-way purgatory; that is, if the sinner is not purified, he will ultimately be consigned to hell. In Shintoism, sins are rubbed on a paper robe and carried out to sea. Such a survey of the world's religions on the subject of salvation underlines the text of Scripture which says, in referring to Jesus Christ, that "there is none other name under heaven given among men, whereby we must be saved."

What do world religions teach about sanctification and ethics? Judaism places great stress on the law, especially as it has been interpreted and elaborated by tradition. Prayer is cultivated, but the great divine dynamic in sanctification is largely lacking. Islam stresses five basic duties: recitation of creed, repetition of prayer five times daily, paying of poor rates, fasting in the month of Ramadan, and the pilgrimage to Mecca. Basically it is externalistic in its conception of ethics, but it does teach the necessity of sincerity. It is against murder but justifies the killing of unbelievers and apostates. It is against adultery and lust but allows four wives, concubinage of slaves, and easy divorce. Sodomy abounds. It is against stealing, requiring that a thief's hands be cut off. Generally, Muslim fatalism undermines ethical concern.

Although the gods of Hinduism are often immoral, this religion has a code forbidding disrespect for parents, the dissolving of marriage, and the breaking of caste. The caste system is probably its greatest moral blemish. It stresses truthfulness, respect for life, and other virtues, but often in an extreme manner. While Hinduism rather takes life as it finds it and even idealizes it, Buddhism condemns life as it finds it and flees it. It seems to tolerate caste while not approving of it, urging its adherents to abandon it and recognize the principle of equality. Though Buddhism advocates a general reverence for life, it has little interest in it, being basically ascetic. It forbids killing, adultery, stealing, lying, and drinking; advocates nonretaliation, and stresses inward motives. Sikhism has more appreciation of individual responsibility, reacting against the deadening effect of the Hindu *karma*. In the same spirit it rejects caste, but the system is far from dead within it. It favors monogamy and abstinence from drink.

Confucianism excels in matters of ethics since it regards religion itself as really nothing but morality. Its leading concept is that of the superman who incarnates all the virtues. He practices the "silver rule," filial piety, and other duties for the duties' sake without ulterior motives. Rulers especially are expected to cultivate virtue. Taoism is the system of poise and power. Inaction is the ideal; it keeps the person in harmony with the Tao and undisturbed by circumstances, such as evil deeds (for which he returns good) or war (into which he would not be drawn or from which he would be protected). In spite of this relatively high ideal, Taoist priests have been distinguished for vice. Like the early Germans, early Japanese had a set of natural virtues. They could not take their cue from the gods, who were often obscene. Nor were prayers designed to secure aid from them but were merely for purposes of conversation. For centuries the prevailing pattern has been the Bushido, or feudalistic, nationalistic loyalty code.

We now make a brief comparison of the teaching of the world religions with respect to the judgment and the world to come. A large number of Jews have become "liberal" and "reformed" and therefore have tended to foreshorten the judgment, restricting it largely to this world. The Orthodox Jews have remained closer to the Old Testament and thereby to the orthodox Christian view. Islam places great emphasis on the day of judgment. Before this event, Jesus will return together with the Imam Mahdi, the expected Messiah, and the resurrection will take place. Men's actions will be weighed in the balance. Lightweights (non-Muslims) will be cast into hell forever. Good Muslims will be in heaven, bad ones in Johannam. The Koran gives vivid descriptions of such corporeal punishments in hell as the drinking of scalding water. It gives an equally corporeal conception of heaven where believers eat special food and have the company of black-eyed houris.

Hinduism gives a strictly circular, not linear, view of history. There is no climax or purpose toward which all nature tends, but only endless repetitions. Incredibly long cycles of transmigrations are in store with the average person expected to undergo about 8,400,000. Heaven and hell are not permanent. Only *karma* abides, and it calls for constant and almost endless transmigrations. Buddhism says that "evildoers go to hell, righteous people go to heaven, and those who are free from all worldly desires attain nirvana." But heaven and hell are not permanent; neither is the person who enjoys the one or endures the other. Although Confucius advocated ancestor worship, which rather implied that the departed spirits survive death, he had no explicit eschatology. As he was agnostic about the gods, so he was agnostic about a possible afterlife with them. He would not inquire into death, he said, until he fully understood life. Taoism seems to teach the purgatorial doctrine. Man's soul goes to purgatory. If it is reformed there, it goes to heaven, but if not, it goes to hell. Under Chinese influence, Shintoism came to reverence departed ancestors, who rivaled the gods in esteem. Accordingly, "man is in this life kindred to the divine and after death joins the company of those who are to be reverenced."

Let us try to form a general comparison of the religions of the world. There are various elements which they have in common. All have something to say about God, even if He be many, on the one hand, or nonexistent as a person, on the other. Man is seen as a moral and personal being. All religions have some sense of the existence of wrongdoing or sin. And likewise they say something about the problem of sin and its cure, even if this cure is merely "doing right." All religions are concerned more or less with morals and have more or less elaborate codes of ethics and are more or less lofty in their conceptions of duty, especially of man's duty to man. All, with the possible exception of Confucianism which may be regarded as relying on original Chinese religion to supply this want, give some idea of the future and make some suggestions about preparing for it. In a word, all religions are religious; that is, they give some view, more or less complete, of this world and the next in relation to God and to the duty of man.

The deficiences of the world's religions in comparison with Christianity are also apparent. Some of them we have observed; a great many more could be noted. But we are not concerned here with the details so much as we are with the great differences. For one thing, only those three religions which stem directly from the Bible have an adequate view of the very being of the God who reveals Himself in all that He has made. Second, only Christianity gives an account of the origin of sin which actually explains the existence of this aberration of which all men and religions are conscious. Likewise, and most important of all, Christianity alone presents a plan of salvation which takes into consideration the nature of a holy God, the depth of human sin and guilt, and the sanctity of the moral law. Fourth, while the religions of the world have some points of resemblance to Christianity in the ethical area, in three ways they are noticeably inferior: their understanding of duty lacks in comprehensiveness and intensiveness; they lack a perfect, personal embodiment of the moral ideal; they lack the dynamic of an indwelling person who makes the commandment come alive. Fifth, as the religions of the world have no adequate view of God, of the nature of sin, or of the requisites of a just salvation, so too they have no adequate teaching about the future, no adequate sense of the nature and work of the day of judgment, no adequate sense of the necessity and awfulness of the judgment of hell, and no adequate sense of the basis for or the majesty of the rewards of an eternal heaven.

The question now arises: What is the fate of non-Christians? Suppose we face this question in its most acute form, namely, the fate of those non-Christians who have never even heard of Christ.[1]

Whatever their culture or country, their unbelief in Christ is circumstantial; that is, they have had no opportunity to believe. This fact raises the question about their "fate." If Christ is the only way of salvation and these persons do not so much as know of the existence of Christ, are we to conclude that they cannot possibly have salvation being necessarily lost or damned? If they are damned, is that not unfair and unjust of God inasmuch as they have no opportunity to be saved?

Let us meet the question right where it emerges: Is it not unjust of God to damn a person who has had no opportunity to be saved? Why is it? Assuming that God does damn such persons, why is it unjust of Him to do so simply because they have no opportunity to be saved? If these persons are damned they are damned because they are sinners; they are not damned because they have had opportunity to be saved and have not utilized it. Their opportunity, or the lack of it, has nothing to do with their being damned; they are damned because they are sinners. What is unfair in God's damning sinners? If God damned them because they did not believe the gospel, they could legitimately protest that they had no opportunity to believe the gospel; but, if God damns them for other sins, what does the fact that they did not commit this sin of unbelief in the gospel have to do with it?

Some will say: Granted that God could damn men for the sins

[1] The following discussion is taken from my article, "The Fate of the Heathen," in *A Dictionary of Theology*, Everett Harrison, ed., and reprinted by permission of Baker Book House, Grand Rapids, Mich.

they have committed even though they did not hear the gospel and there would be no injustice in that as such. But, does God not have an obligation to offer a way of salvation to everyone? But, we ask, why? Why does God have any obligation to offer salvation to any sinner? Grace, by definition, is undeserved. If it were deserved, it would not be a gospel; it would not be grace. If it is a gospel of grace it must be undeserved. If it is undeserved how can it be said that God owes it to anyone?

All right, some will reply, but inasmuch as God (who did not owe the gospel to anyone) did give it to many, is He not under obligation to offer it everyone? But why? If a person who does not deserve it receives a gift, does another person who does not deserve it thereby gain a right to a gift? If he does gain a right to it, is it still a "gift" or a "gospel"? But it is further urged, this makes God a respecter of persons. Indeed it does; but the respecter of persons which the Bible condemns is an unfair respecter of persons. God is not an unfair respecter of persons and this is no instance of an unfair discrimination. He gives a gift which He does not owe; that puts Him under no obligation to give a gift, the same gift, to everyone to whom He does not owe it. Being a respecter of persons, if it is a fair discrimination, is not evil. (Cf. the Parable of the Laborers, Matt. 20:1 ff., which speaks to this very point.) "Is it not lawful for me to do what I will with mine own? Is Thine eye evil, because I am good?" (v. 15).

All of the above is by way of facing the objections which are commonly made to the doctrine that the "heathen" are lost. Such, we believe, is the teaching of the Word of God. "Faith cometh by hearing, and hearing by the word of God" is the teaching of Rom. 10:17 in which context the necessity of missionaries is being argued. The world by wisdom knew not God, but it pleased God by the foolishness of preaching to make his wisdom known (I Cor. 1:21). The wrath of God is revealed from heaven against all the unrighteousness of men who hold the truth in unrighteousness but the gospel is the power of God unto salvation to everyone that believeth (Rom. 1:16-18). Christ is the light of the world. All the world is in darkness until he shines into it (John 8:12, 9:5).

There is none other name given under heaven whereby men must be saved but the name of Jesus (Acts 4:12). He is the way, the truth and the life, no man coming to God but by Him (John 14:6).

Christ, in teaching this doctrine Himself, brings out an aspect of the truth which has not yet been mentioned here. In Luke 12:47, 48 He tells us that the disobedient man who does not know will be beaten with fewer stripes than the disobedient man who does know. That is to say, that those who do not know the gospel are guilty because of the light which they have and which they have transgressed (cf. especially Rom. 1), but they are not so guilty as those who have had the light of the gospel as well as the light of nature and have sinned against that also. Their light having been so much greater their hardness of heart was so much more developed in resisting it and their guilt is much the more grievous. Therefore, according to Matt. 10:15, 11:22, it shall be more tolerable for Sodom and Gomorrah (who are in hell though they sinned only against the light of nature) than for Capernaum and Chorazin (who are in hell with far greater condemnation because they have violated a light so vastly greater than the heathen transgressed).

In conclusion, it may be well to cite the remark of the great Baptist theologian, A. H. Strong: "The question whether the heathen will ever be saved if we do not give them the gospel, is not so serious a one for us as the other question whether we ourselves will ever be saved if we do not give them the gospel." That is to say: Christians have an obligation to evangelize the world. If they do not actively participate in that duty, although some persons may be lost through their negligence, they will perish with them and with far greater punishment because they have themselves sinned against the far greater light which they have had. In other words, the "fate" of the "heathen" is inextricably connected with the "fate" of "Christians."

17

The Influence of Christianity (1)

SHORTLY before his death, Jesus said, "Believe me for my very works' sake. Verily, verily I say unto you, greater works than these shall ye do." They were very ordinary men to whom Christ, admittedly the most extraordinary person ever to appear in human history, spoke these words. Strange prediction that. Stranger still that it has been fulfilled. Stranger still how it has been fulfilled.

If Jesus meant that His disciples would do greater miracles than He, it certainly has not happened. If there have been any bona fide miracles at all, in the sense of events wrought in the external world by the immediate power of God without the use of second causes, they have not been as great as those of the Master. Certainly they have not been greater. The most that can even be claimed is a wonder of healing here and another there usually on the part of the lesser men rather than the greater men of the Church. But nowhere do any even claim to multiply loaves and fishes. None blight fig trees. And who has walked on water, raised the dead, or been raised from the dead?

But there is an area in which the disciples have done the great works of the Master—and greater works.

First, they have done greater works for the bodies of men. When Christ uttered this prophecy, infanticide was a common thing. Quintilian and others regarded it as a beautiful custom to abandon infants. It was the followers of Jesus who had said, "Suffer the little children to come unto me and forbid them not," who put an end to this "beautiful custom." Clement, Origen, and Tertullian, the fathers of the Church, exposed the horror of it. The weakest of all creatures, the human infant, became the best protected of all as the followers of Jesus continued to much greater lengths the emancipation of childhood. As James Stalker has written:

[Christ] converted the home into a church, and parents into His ministers; and it may be doubted whether He has not by this means won to Himself as many disciples in the course of the Christian ages as even by the institution of the church itself.

Murder for pleasure was eradicated by the disciples of Christ. When Jesus uttered the promise about greater works, the Romans regarded gladiatorial combats as the choicest of amusements. And the bloodier the battle of condemned slaves or captives, the rarer the diversion. Telemachus leaped into the arena in order to separate the warriors but succeeded only in having himself stoned by an enraged mob of spectators to whom he was only a mad spoilsport. He was of course, a Christian. He died, but gladiatorial combats were to die with him as the Church went on to do greater works in this area than her Founder.

It may be well for us to remember the background against which these transformations took place. To get an insight into Christianity's contribution to Roman moral culture generally we need only remember what that culture was at the time Christianity reached it.

The Colosseum was called the "most characteristic relic of Pagan Rome." In each of twelve spectacles given by Aediles, from one hundred to five hundred pairs of gladiators appeared, to fight to the death with net, dagger, lances and trident, or with straight or curved blades, ground to the finest edge and point. At the triumph of Aurelian, later, eight hundred pairs of gladiators fought ten thousand men during the games of Trajan. Sometimes female gladiators fought, sometimes dwarfs, as under Domitian. And the condemned were sometimes burned in shirts of pitch to illuminate the gardens, or were hung on crosses and left to be torn by famished bears before the populace. The combats of animals, with each other or with men, was always refreshing to this horrid thirst for cruel excitement. Criminals, dressed in the skins of wild beasts, were exposed to tortured and maddened bulls. Under Nero, four hundred tigers fought with elephants and bulls. At the dedication of the Colosseum, by Titus, five thousand animals were killed. The rhinoceros, the hippo, the stag, the giraffe, even the crocodile and the serpent were introduced in what Tertullian fitly called "this Devil's pomp" and there is scarcely one element of horror, which can be conceived in man's wildest dreams, which was not presented as a matter of luxury to make complete the "Roman holiday" at the time when Christianity entered the capital.

Christianity has a chequered record with respect to slavery. It has not always stood for abolition. But it has always taught amelioration. The New Testament clearly permitted slavery, but only with the master and the subject both brothers in Christ. In an empire which was literally half slave and half free with an unbridgeable gulf between, such brotherhood was drastic. And when a noble Christian, Perpetua, bent over and kissed her slave girl before both were gored to death as Christian martyrs, she was kissing the institution of slavery good-by. When a bondman became a bishop of Rome, it was becoming quite apparent that there were neither bond nor free in Christ. When Negro slavery again raised its head in modern times, it was banished from the British Empire by the relentless persistence of a Christ-motivated Wilberforce.

And while the churches in the United States did not always stand unequivocally for abolition, there is no question that, as Beardsley remarks,

It must be admitted that the Church as an organization had little to do directly in bringing about this result, yet we must never forget that behind the public events and issues of the time there was the moral consciousness of the American people which was a determining factor in this mighty conflict. Slavery met its deathblow at the hands of a Christian civilization, and but for a quickened Christian consciousness this withering curse might still be upon us.

What George Washington Carver said of the Methodist Simmons College, which he attended, could be said of Christian institutions generally: "It was the place where I first discovered that I was a human being." And speaking of the Methodists, we are reminded that Henry Clay, when he heard that the Methodist Episcopal Church had split over slavery, went white in his face as he exclaimed, "My God, that means war."

To take but one other example, consider cannibalism. Of all the atrocious deeds of man against man the most gruesome is cannibalism. With this practice of degenerate savagery Christ had no personal contact, yet its abolition is the work of those who, in His name, have done greater works than He. When a South Pacific islander told a European mocker of foreign missions that if it had not been for the missionaries the mocker would not be alive to say that he did not believe in missions, he was true to the record. It was through missionaries, a number of whom actually became the victims of this hideous cannibalism, that it has been almost entirely exterminated. Many a soldier in World War II subsequently told of his amazement to find himself welcomed rather than devoured in some remote island where he had been stranded. How glad were weary men, trudging through the jungles fearful of what the next clearing would reveal, to see Christian churches and know that they were safe. These were the experiences which made missionaries of GI's and produced the now famous "khaki viewpoint." They found the Church there where the disciples were doing greater works than their Lord.

While we are speaking about barbaric customs, let us mention in passing what Christianity has done for barbaric peoples generally. Christlieb was one of the most comprehensive students of missions among primitive peoples. He tells us, among many other things, what Christ has done for the Hottentots.

Until within thirty years, one might express a doubt as to whether the gospel could elevate and heal the most degraded heathen, and prove a savor of life unto life. But to-day the Portuguese can no longer maintain that the Hottentots are a race of apes, incapable of Christianization. You can no longer find written over church doors in Cape Colony, "Dogs and Hottentots not admitted," as at the time when Dr. Van der Kemp fought there for the rights of the downtrodden natives. To-day no one could be found to agree with the French governor of the island of Bourbon, who called out to the first missionary to Madagascar, "So you will make the Malagasy Christians? Impossible! they are mere brutes, and have no more sense than irrational cattle"; since there are hundreds of evangelical congregations established there. . . .

Warneck was another great student of primitive cultures and the impact of missions upon them. His many studies and researches in field and literature led him to this conclusion: "It is well known that the similar ring of the words 'religion' (the German is "Cultus") and 'culture' is not accidental. As they stem etymologically from the same root, so they do in the sphere of life which they indicate have a common organic relationship." That is to say, culture is the product of cultus.

Civilization has never been produced by anything other than religion. And no society which has once lapsed into barbarism has ever been known to rise to civilization except by the Christian religion.

Hospitals for the sick and dying? The pre-Christian world had not heard of them. The most that could be said was that there were, in some places, shelters for the shipwrecked. We do not mean to suggest that there were no humane people in pagan antiquity. There were the noble Stoics: Epictetus, Cicero, Aurelius. They knew to give charity and they gave it, but they did not know how to give it. The Stoic "stands aloof and thinks what these deeds will bring him." Epictetus says, "Now another's grief is no concern of mine, but my own grief is."

Charity was known, but hardly love. Surely not *agape* love, not love which gives where there is no merit and can be no hope of return. On a greater scale than the Master ever had done it, the disciples gave without letting their right hand know what their left hand was doing. Cicero wrote:

We should weigh with discrimination the worthiness of the object of our benevolence; we should take into consideration his moral character, his attitude toward us, the intimacy of his relation to us, and our social ties, as well as the services he has hitherto rendered in our interest.

Contrast this with Christian charity. As Storrs has well stated the matter:

Philosophers had sometimes suggested the sovereignty of the human sentiments as a remote and delightful ideal; but what has been truly called by one of their admirers their "reasoned and passionless philanthropy" has had no power to solace sorrow, to relieve labor, to comfort the poor, to inspire or quicken despondent souls. Now came a law of charity to mankind: believed to have been incarnated in the Christ, warmly welcomed and ardently realized by his followers; which sought the weary, the needy and the sick; which knew no bounds of race or tongue, which prayed for even the judge who sentenced and the savage executioner whose blade struck the blow. When the archdeacon Laurentius was called upon by the prefect of the city for the treasures of the (Roman) church, he presented under the colonades the poor, the crippled and the sick, whom this had sheltered and nourished.

It is not sufficient to notice that the disciples of Christ learned from Him to give from unearned love and thus to alleviate the pitiable suffering of an inhumane humanity. For the first time in history, we meet with an effort to cure the cause of need as well as relieve the effects of it. Ulhorn, after an extensive survey of the charity of ancient Rome and a glance at the new element introduced by Christianity, observes that for the first time in history a systematic and curative charity was practiced, a charity which ministered to need in a way that tended to make itself unnecessary.

Nor has Christianity stopped with a ministry to the bodies of men. It has gone on to care even for animals. Professor Addison H. Leitch, of Pittsburgh-Xenia Theological Seminary, says that for him a clear indication of the relative superiority of a Christian culture is seen in a comparison of the horses which he saw in Egypt with those in Christian lands. Anything like a Society for the Prevention of Cruelty to Animals outside an evangelized nation, we have never heard of. Rogers calls to our attention that "what is probably the first instance of legislation for their protection was due to Constantine, who ordered that only light rods or goads with short harmless points were to be used for horses used in public service, and that they were not to be overdriven (Decree, May 14, A.D. 316, P.L. VIII, Col. 142)."

18

The Influence of Christianity (2)

THE disciples of Christ have done much for the bodies of men and beasts, but a great deal more for the minds of men. Nor have they forgotten those whose minds function abnormally. The first insane asylum, in the proper sense of the word, was the gift to the world of William Tuke, a Quaker. Before that, the hospital had not been unaware of the special needs of these unfortunates.

But since the majority of mankind have adequate minds, the primary ministry of Christendom has been to these. In general, education is, as has often been said, the handmaid of religion. Where the Church has gone, the school has always followed her, occasionally preceded her. Americans, especially, know that every school of higher learning on the colonial seaboard and generally everywhere else has been established, in the first instance, by the Church. There is one apparent exception. The University of Pennsylvania was not established by the Church but came into being largely through the efforts of Benjamin Franklin. It is well to remember, however, that even in this case the founder acknowledged that the impetus toward the building of the original academy came from his evangelist friend, George Whitefield.

It was no longer necessary for the Church to foster the schools when the state, which was largely nurtured by the Church, awoke to her responsibilities. And so, many schools are now secular which were once maintained by religion. It is significant to see, however, that the Christian Church the world over maintains about as many schools as churches even today.

And what of the "silent billions"—those who cannot speak their needs and demands because they cannot read or write? What about the illiterate other half? Who is teaching them to read, to write, and to articulate their wants? Everyone knows the name of Frank Laubach and his famous "each one teach one" method. But does everyone know that he is constrained in this great service to mankind by the love of Christ? And does everyone know that his chief agents, unpaid agents, are the far-flung missionaries of the cross?

From the barbarian invasions to the present time, Christ's disciples have been building schools for the minds of men. But no less important than giving men schools to attend is to give them reasons for attending. It is not enough to have a place to study if there is no incentive to mental effort, which is admittedly a "weariness to the flesh." It is far more important, therefore, although far less conspicuous, that the Church has given not only places in which to study but a reason for studying.

What is the Christian reason for studying? As the Heidelberg Catechism puts it, "nature is the book of God." Elementary children in Christian schools are taught that history is "His story." Psychology studies the laws of the mind which He has made, and literature the works of genius which He has given to all mankind. Christianity knows of only two sources of knowledge, special and common revelation. Special revelation is the supernatural disclosure which God has made of Himself and His redemption in the Bible. Common revelation is the natural revelation which God has made of Himself in the ordinary constitution of nature and human affairs. Both of these are revelation by and of God. Both lead to a knowledge of God. If that be so, what Christian will not be willing, indeed eager, to study?

Some psychologist has stated that the average person does not use more than 10 per cent of his intelligence potential. The problem back of all problems is therefore how to get men to use the ability which God has given them for the solving of problems. Is not the assurance that man has the privilege and duty of thinking God's thoughts after Him sufficient incentive for anyone? And has anyone ever been intellectually lazy who has thus sincerely believed? True religion, far from being activity merely of the emotions, is the most powerful possible inducement to ratiocination.

Consider, on the other hand, the effect of unbelief on scholarship. Suppose, for example, that the generality of men believed that the exact sciences were merely games (Abel), that nothing was worthwhile except art, sex, and a few other tangible pleasures (Dreiser), and that the beginning and end of thought was complete and unyielding despair (Bertrand Russell). Would they continue attending school? The world would play hookey. Men may study if they do not know at the outset that the search will lead up a blind alley, or they may study though it be intellectually unrewarding but financially remunerative. But why else will they study? It is not only, as Augustine said, that the human heart is restless till it finds its rest in God, but the human mind as well.

We could fill this volume and many more besides by merely listing without comment the names of the great thinkers of the world who have been motivated by the gospel. Everyone knows Kepler's famous statement that he, in his astronomical research, was merely thinking God's thoughts after Him. Jonathan Edwards, who is regarded by many as the finest intelligence America ever produced and whose *Inquiry into the Freedom of Will* is often called the best piece of purely logical writing in existence, was intellectually a slave of the Bible. The noted French discoverer of bacteria was once bending over his microscope when his assistant came in, and, supposing him to be praying, the assistant began to tiptoe out of the room. When Pasteur hear him and looked up, the assistant said that he was sorry; he had thought Dr. Pasteur was at devotions. Pasteur replied, "I was at devotions." Sir Alexander Fleming, the discoverer of penicillin, once remarked that the almost accidental character of his discovery had reminded him of nothing so much as the doctrine of divine foreordination in which he had been reared in his Scottish home.

And greater works than these have Christ's disciples done for the souls of men. First, their gospel has cleansed the guilt of men's souls. Guilt is written large in the hearts of men, a guilt felt toward someone greater than the finite person against whom the offense has been immediately committed. "Against thee and thee only have I sinned." Men who deny the very existence of God with their lips seem to tremble before Him in their hearts. As Calvin writes, "The most audacious contemners of God are most alarmed, even at the noise of a falling leaf." So it is that we have the rather familiar phenomenon that godless people become keenly aware of their sins when they suppose that death is upon them. A character in one of Ernest Hemingway's novels—an especially immoral sort—is asked if he never thinks of God. The reply is that he does sometimes—in the middle of the night when he is awakened by a thunderstorm. The predicament, which all seem to share with Lady Macbeth, of being unable to wash out the cursed spot of guilt, lies at the base of all man's griefs. Nor will it do to deny the reality of this guilt-consciousness or its significance. The cursed spot is there and it will not out until the evangel tells:

> There is a fountain filled with blood
> Drawn from Emanuel's veins
> And sinners plunged beneath that flood
> Lose all their guilty stains.

It is a fact repeated a billion times over that when the sinner loaded with his burden of guilt catches sight of the cross, he experiences the same deliverance which Bunyan's pilgrim knew—his burdens roll from his back to disappear forever.

The Gospel of Christ has brought not only cleansing from guilt, but also power in place of weakness. We read in many volumes on sociology, psychology, and education that the prime need of our time is in the area of motivation. We hear a philosopher say this: "If I could always think what is true and do what is right, I would be willing to be turned into some sort of a clock." An educator remarks: "We need someone who can make virtue more attractive than vice." Innumerable statesmen speak like this one: "Our greatest need is theological."

We have known all this for a long time, but when the atom bomb fell, the truth seemed to thunder in our ears: "Spiritual man is not keeping pace with mechanical man"; "We have a man who can make a bomb, where can we find someone who can make a man?" Democracy is a great ideal but who can make the ideal work? Right is right but who can make a person always love and do the right?

Harold Begbie, the famous author of the documentary study of the London slums, *Twice-Born Men,* gives this testimony:

When I visit the happy homes, and experience the gentleness and refinement of such as those whose life stories appear in this book, and compare them with the squalor and misery of the great majority of homes surrounding them, I am astonished that the world should be incredulous about religion, and that legislation should be so foolish as to attempt to do laboriously by enactments, clumsy and slow, what might be done instantly and easily by religion if it had the full force of the community back of it.

The writer of this book has never lived in a slum but he has the same testimony. Of himself alone he is selfish, lustful, proud, lazy, greedy, foolish, vicious, vain, deceitful . . . He knows that the only reason—the *only* reason—he is not that way all the time and altogether is Jesus Christ. He knows that if he ever is sincerely unselfish, ever wholesome, ever humble, ever industrious, ever generous, ever wise, ever gentle, ever sober, ever honest . . . it is because of Jesus Christ and Him alone. And he knows that there are millions of people in the world now who are just like him and would give exactly the same witness.

Ye hath he quickened who were dead in trespasses and sins; wherein time past ye walked according to the course of this world, according to the prince of the power of the air, the spirit that now worketh in the children of disobedience; among whom also we all had our conversation in times past in the lusts of our flesh, fulfilling the desires of the flesh and of the mind; and were by nature the children of wrath, even as others. But God, who is rich in mercy, for his great love wherewith he loved us, even when we were dead in sins, hath quickened us together with Christ. . . .

And the evangelists of Christ have brought joy to the hearts of men. The symphony of this world is written in a minor key. Perhaps it is no accident that while Aristotle has been accepted as a satisfactory definer of tragedy, no one has been able to tell what comedy is. We know tragedy better than comedy. The Germans have a word for it—*Weltschmerz*—which all the world understands. The great philosopher Schopenhauer, mistaken for a bum in a Berlin park, was reprimanded by a policeman who asked, "Who do you think you are?" Sadly he replied, "I would to God I knew." Some unknown, a philosopher in his own right, said essentially the same thing. Asked why he drank so much, he answered, "To get out of Hoboken for two hours." But it isn't Hoboken from which men want to escape. Their hearts are their Hobokens; they don't want to be alone with their own hearts. And so they make themselves happy by rendering themselves unconscious of their grief—for awhile.

It takes a Shakespeare to describe the miseries of men, but it takes a Christ to bear them. "Come unto me, all ye that labor and are heavy laden, and I will give you rest. . . . learn of me; for I am meek and lowly in heart: and ye shall find rest unto your souls."

The argument from joy is one of the greatest arguments for Christianity. It is invulnerable and overwhelming. No one who professes to know Jesus Christ as his Saviour and Lord will deny that he is happy—profoundly happy, blessed. Whether he is rich or poor, whether he is talented or mediocre, whether he is sick or well, whether he lives or dies, if he is in Christ Jesus, he will say with Paul, "Rejoice, and again I say rejoice." So impressed was Dr. Wilbur Smith with this argument from joy that in his *Therefore Stand* he ranged it right alongside the resurrection of Christ as a fundamental fact certifying the divinity of the Christian religion. Listen to the voices of redeemed men:

> Bernard of Clairvaux—
> Jesus, the very thought of Thee
> With sweetness fills my breast . . .

> Robert Robinson:
> Come, Thou Fount of every blessing,
> Tune my heart to sing Thy grace;

Streams of mercy, never ceasing,
Call for songs of loudest praise.

John Keble:
Sun of my soul, Thou Saviour dear,
It is not night if Thou be near . . .

Isaac Watts:
Alas! and did my Saviour bleed,
And did my Sovereign die!
Would He devote that sacred head
For sinners such as I!

19

The Argument from Experience

As WE come to the argument from experience, we must first have some understanding of what experience is. More than two hundred definitions have been given to this elusive concept. It does not behoove us here to go into a technical discussion but merely to ascertain a working definition that will be sound if not exhaustive.

Speaking very broadly, experience is a nonphysical reaction to ideas, a reaction which may or may not have physical consequences. We will not raise the question whether there are physical stimuli which produce physical responses without any intermediary ideas. Rather, we are concerned with that variety of experience which is a reaction to some notion or idea. To be specific, when we read of a young serviceman dashing through a crowd of spectators to rescue three men injured in a turned-over and burning auto, the fact comes to our minds in the form of a concept or notion or idea or understanding. It is of the nature of man that when these ideas enter his mind, they do not stop there. They produce some inner response. The response may vary with individuals or with the same individual at different times. The unvarying factor is the invariability of the response. That is, no one could see the event to which we have referred, hear of it, read of it, or by any means know of it, without having some response. The response may be one of admiration, pity, or scorn; or it may be scorn at first turning to admiration later; or it may be scorn in one person and admiration in another. But there will be some response of some sort in every person. This response is usually called feeling or emotion.

Feeling or emotion is dependent on the idea but it is not identical with it. Unless a person has some idea he has no feeling. Feeling is a response to an idea. This feeling is experience in the narrower sense of the word, the sense with which we are now concerned.

Emotions or feelings are of two kinds, pleasant and unpleasant. That feeling is good for a man which in a given situation tends to bring him most true and lasting benefit. A pleasant feeling is not necessarily good for him; an unpleasant feeling is not necessarily bad for him. The value of the feeling depends on the situation of the man who has it.

For example, for a man to have the pleasant emotion of joy when he is dangerously ill may not be good for him. Because of such a feeling at such a time and with respect to such a condition, he may neglect the care of his sickness and die. Instead, it may be good for the man if he have the unpleasant feeling of fear. Fear would lead him to concern, which would cause him to treat his malady and possibly cure it.

It may appear from the above illustration that feelings have no character of their own, but are solely dependent on their relation to other things. It would not be correct to jump to that conclusion. Feelings are indeed related to other matters which have a distinct bearing on their value. Still, feelings also have a character and importance all their own. Thus it is good, everything else being equal, for a man to have joy rather than fear. Fear in and of itself tends to destroy the man physically and mentally, while joy is a proper medium for the living of the good and suitable life. Fear is a liability, but it may be justified in a given instance if it prevents a greater liability, leading one to a course of action which will remove both the peril and the fear and ultimately bring about joy. So that the only positive value of a feeling such as fear is as a function of joy or an indirect way to joy or a way of avoiding a still further removal from joy.

Now let us see what is the bearing of these feelings on Christianity, or the bearing of Christianity on these feelings. Christianity produces different feelings in different persons and different feelings in the same person at different times. Are these effects of Christianity the right effects or the wrong ones? If they are the right effects then we have an argument from experience, for it stands to reason that the God who made men would do those things which were suited to the condition of the men he made. If therefore these experiential effects of Christianity are fitted to the states of men, we have confirmation that they are from God. If they are not suited, the indication is that they are not from God.

First, the effect of Christianity on man as he now is, before anything such as conversion happens to him, is frightening. The gospel says to him, in the words of Jesus, "except ye repent ye shall all likewise perish." It warns him to "flee from the wrath to come." "The wages of sin," the Bible warns, "is death." "The way of the wicked shall perish." God calls men everywhere to repent, for he has appointed a time to judge the world by the man Christ Jesus whom He raised from the dead. "It is appointed unto men once to die, and after this judgment." It confirms the consciences of men that God is a holy God, of purer eyes than to behold iniquity, who will by no means clear the guilty. "Whatsoever a man soweth, that shall he also reap." This distinctly disturbs the peace of mind, and the Bible specifically warns against peace of mind which is not based on a new mind in Christ. It deplores those who cry "peace, peace, when there is no peace," and says, through Amos, that the day of light which men expect is going to be a day of darkness.

Such a feeling as fear is not good in itself. It is unpleasant, uncongenial, and unsuited to the proper existence of a man, as we have said. But when man is exposed to such danger as the judgment of the holy God, fear is the feeling he most desperately needs. The greater his fear, the better it will be for the man. On the other hand, to feel joy under such circumstances would be the worst possible experience. The fear, though unwelcome, is proper and sound; the joy, though welcome, would be spurious and unsound. His fear is based on fact and may lead to favorable consequences; his joy would be based on illusion and would lead to ruin.

Fear can be paralyzing. We read of victims of the ancient hordes of Genghis Khan who were so frightened by the barbarians that all their resistance melted, and they willingly submitted themselves to extermination. Now the terror of the Lord is infinitely more awful than that of any man. So the question arises whether this fear which the serious consideration of Christianity would beget in the heart of a rational but fallen being is not also, and still more, paralyzing and therefore destructive rather than helpful.

The fact is that Christianity would be paralyzing if it contained nothing but this premonition of doom. But such is not at all the case. The warning is merely a prelude to the Christian message, an introduction, a point of contact. "I came not," said Christ, "to condemn the world but that the world through me might be saved." Christianity is a Gospel, it is good news. That men will perish forever if they live and die in their sins is not news, and certainly it is not good news. But Christianity is a proclamation that "God so loved the world that he gave his only begotten Son that whosoever believeth on him should not perish but have everlasting life." This Gospel tells of grace, or unmerited favor, whereby a God who had no obligation to any man except to damn him, offered instead only sheer and disinterested love, giving His dear Son to suffer the torments of the damned. Therefore the repentant one is able to say, through faith, "I am persuaded, that neither death, nor life, nor angels, nor principalities, nor powers, nor things present, nor things to come, nor height, nor depth, nor any other creature, shall be able to separate us from the love of God, which is in Christ Jesus our Lord."

Thus Christianity produces the feeling suitable to an unconverted man—utter fear. But at the same time it is not a paralyzing fear, for the Gospel holds out hope to him, not only of escape from a just and impending doom, but of life and blessedness as infinite and glorious as the terror of the Lord is infinite and awesome.

But consider the joy of the person who repents and believes this gospel. His burdens roll from his back. He finds rest for his soul. There is peace. Love flows through his very being. These are pleasant emotions and they are eminently and manifestly suited to the perfect existence of a human being. Nor are they specious, based on ignorance, but real, based on truth. The unconverted may cry "peace, peace" (and even succeed in inducing the feeling of it), but there is no real peace. When, however, the reconciled cry "peace," they speak truth. The wish is not father to the thought; the truth is father to the experience.

There is a manifest hazard here. Suppose someone fancies that by saying he believes this, he may have an easy way out of all his fears. What is to prevent hypocrites from taking full advantage of the Gospel and securing an easy peace based apparently on truth? The Gospel itself prevents it. It solemnly warns men that those who merely pretend to repent, are exposed to still more of the anger of God than those who are outwardly wicked with no pretenses to augment their guilt. Woe to those who are "at ease in Zion." Those who cast out one such devil only make place for seven others.

So every precaution is found in Christianity against the appearance of any false faith and deluded security. Men are to examine themselves whether they are in Christ Jesus or whether they are reprobates (II Cor. 13:5).

But as soon as we note that one danger is carefully marked by Christianity, we wonder about its opposite. Granted that no one can properly come to a superficial security if he follows the rules of the Christian faith. Granted that the Bible requires men to examine themselves and to work out their own salvation with fear and trembling. Will this humbling of the spirit not tend to produce a morbid introspectiveness in serious Christians? Will they not always be pulling up the new plant to find out if it is growing? Will they not be haunted with fears that they are not truly Christians? In other words, will Christianity not make Christians, of all men, most miserable? And the more Christian they become, the more miserable will they not also become? And so will Christian experience not be a very sad experience?

No, Christianity has safeguarded against that hazard also, and most wonderfully so. It assures the person that if he have faith as of a grain of mustard seed, he shall be able to move mountains. Not a perfect and strong faith is required for assurance, but the very minimum. Christianity commands a person to be no less than perfect, but it assures him, at the same time, that if he does not attain this ideal while striving for it, God is gracious to forgive his sins and through the blood of Christ to cleanse him from all unrighteousness. Jesus constantly rebuked His disciples for having little faith. He called them children and said that there were many things which He would have told them but which they could not bear. All these were rebukes to be sure, but they were the rebukes of a loving father whose children knew that they were loved. So it always is with Christ. He demands the most complete discipleship. If any man would come after Him, he must take up his cross and follow Him even to the death. But at the same time, if the disciple's heart is right and he is truly endeavoring after discipleship, the Master is most concessive to his weaknesses. Thus it becomes possible for a Christian to have assurance of his Saviour's favor without the slightest temptation to presume upon that favor or fancy that he may rely upon it while ceasing to strive after a perfect obedience. So Christianity gives the most exacting moral imperative, produces the deepest humility, and at the same time provides the greatest possible assurance.

All that has so far been mentioned of Christian experience is the experience of the Christian which flows from a sound understanding of Christian truth. Nothing as yet has been said of the experience which comes from communion with a person. But this is the heart of Christian experience. Not the joy which flows from obedience to principles, but the joy which springs up from within by the indwelling of the Lord of life Himself. Jesus represents Himself as standing at the door of the heart of a man and offering to come in and sup with him (Rev. 3:20). He promises that not only He, but the Father as well, will come and live in the heart of the believer. He promises never to leave nor forsake the servant who is faithful to His command. He tells men that He is the bread of life of which if a man eat, he shall never hunger again; that he is the water of life of which if a man drink, he shall never thirst. He promises to be to believing souls as a well of water springing up unto eternal life. He tells His disciples that they must eat His flesh and drink His blood if they would have life. By this simile He makes it very plain that He Himself will be united to the soul of true believers. He likens Himself to the vine to which His disciples are grafted and from which they receive their life and vitality.

The apostle Paul explains the intimacy and vitality of this union of the Christian with Christ. "For to me," he says, "to live is Christ" (Phil. 1:21). That is to say, Jesus Christ dwelling in him became the principle of his living, his motivation. While his own individuality was by no means destroyed, it was certainly transformed so that not his old sinful self was the basis of his motivation, but the living Christ within him. He expresses the same truth even more profoundly in the Galatian letter. "I am crucified with Christ: nevertheless I live; yet not I, but Christ liveth in me: and the life which I now live in the flesh I live by the faith of the Son of God, who loved me, and gave himself for me" (2:20). He had been crucified or destroyed with Christ, but in such a way that he still continued to live, but in an entirely new and different manner. The Christ who died for him now lived in him. And the life that he lived out, as it were, was the expression through him of the Christ who was the foundation of his new and true life. All his life was faith in the Son of God. Thus for him death was gain, because it assured him of a still fuller manifestation of the presence of Christ, which in its lesser measure now was still his very life and all his joy.

That which makes Christian experience most joyous is not what it is, but what it is yet to be. "All this and heaven too." "We rejoice in hope of the glory of God" (Rom. 5:2). Christians confidently anticipate their fullness of joy in the world to come. Jonathan Edwards has written that the joy of the coming world so much transcends the joy of this world that by comparison this will appear to the saint as a veritable hell; just as the anguish of the coming world will be so terrible to the wicked that this present world will then seem to him like heaven.

Even the anticipation of this joy is joy. Merely thinking about the wonders of heaven is pleasant in itself. It fills the soul with wonder and blessedness. It is a foretaste, as if heaven were sending messengers to prepare men for the splendors of the invisible world. Communism is always taunting Christianity with teaching its adherents that there will be "pie in the sky by-and-by." It is true that Christianity does teach that there will be rewards in the world to come, but it teaches more than that. It teaches that there is for the Christian "pie" here and now. Christian experience is a present reality. Believers now possess a peace which passes understanding, a joy which the world can neither give nor take away, a communion with the Lord of glory which shines more and more to the perfect day. At the same time that the Christian does not have to wait until death to enter into the joy of his Lord, he knows that at death he will enter far more fully into that joy.

20

The Witness of the Martyrs

NOTHING proves a man's attachment to a thing so surely as his readiness to die for it. "Skin for skin," said Browning, "all a man hath that will he give for life." "Greater love hath no man than this, that a man lay down his life for his friend," said Jesus. It is self-evident that the most precious possession which any man has is himself. He is more than his possessions, and if he will give his life, that is prima-facie evidence that the end for which he gives it is of supreme value to him. A man may give his life for something that is trifling indeed, but he cannot give his life for something that seems trifling to him. To do so would prove him to be a nonrational being, or something other than he is.

Nevertheless, as we have intimated, that for which a man gives his life is not necessarily valuable. It may only seem valuable to him at the moment. It itself may be trifling; indeed it may be sinful. For example, there is every reason to believe that some people have given themselves for their pride. They do not care to have other persons tell them what to do; they would rather die than permit it. The doing of what they want to do seems to them more important than the thing itself. If they cannot do what they want, then they will do nothing. We would say that this attitude is the mark of a spoiled baby, but the fact is that it has its martyrs. "No one is going to tell me what to do," is not essentially a right frame of mind; there are many instances when others must tell us what to do. Children must be told by their parents; pupils must be told by their teachers; privates must be told by their superiors what to do. It may be well that we should not permit someone else to tell us to do certain things; indeed we may have to refuse even if the refusal involves death. But then we are not refusing on the ground that "no one is going to tell me what to do," but on the ground that the thing demanded is morally wrong. There is a great difference, the difference between an intelligent basis for martyrdom and a spoiled baby complex. But each has had its martyrs.

Even death for religion is not necessarily virtuous. That is, some may die in the name of religion and have none of it. They may give their bodies to be burned and not have love. For what do such persons then die? They die to appear religious. They want to be seen of men, even in death. They want the adulation of the crowd who admire such apparent heroism for the faith.

Other men die for superstition. They draw a knife through their own bowels and are beheaded as they fall forward because they think that their gods require such actions on certain occasions. We pity such persons rather than admire them. But we cannot doubt that that for which they are willing to give their very lives means much to them—more than anything else, including themselves.

So then we must qualify our conception of martyrdom. A true martyrdom or a martyrdom that is admirable must be death for truth. If death is incurred for something other than truth, necessary truth, it is not admirable but pitiable, not courageous but foolhardy.

If, on the other hand, a man holds true principle but not to the death, he is not a fool but a coward, and it is an argument against the principle that it should produce a coward. How can anything be true which none the less does not make truthful characters of its adherents? If it be the truth of God, it must be "unto godliness." So we must conclude one of two things. Either such a person holds the truth in unrighteousness; that is, he pretends to hold it, he nominally holds it but it does not hold him. Or else it is not the truth of God. For if it be the truth of God it will teach that God's will must be supreme; all else, including life, is subordinate to it.

Hence a man may hold the truth and not be a martyr, in which case he does not really hold the truth. Or he may not hold the truth but be a martyr, in which case he is not a martyr but a fool. A martyr is a person who holds the truth and dies for it. If he holds the truth and does not die for it, he is a hypocrite; if he dies for something other than the truth, he is a fool. A martyr is a person who dies for truth, the truth of God.

Granting the definition, what is the record of Christianity with respect to martyrs? What would we expect it to be? In addition to true believers, there are many among its adherents who only nominally understand and belong to it and many who belong for some reasons other than their belief in the truth of this religion and many who are very weak though sincere. We should therefore expect that the fires of persecution would reveal these different classes to be present in the Christian church. That is, we would expect some, precisely because they were adherents for a reason other than their sincere belief in the truth of Christianity, to recant as soon as that ulterior motive was removed. If they belonged to the church because of some secular advantage which such membership may have brought, they would of course abandon their faith as soon as that advantage was lost. And certainly the threatening of their lives would be a threat to all of their worldly interest. Nominal attachment to Christianity could not be expected to survive such an ordeal. We would expect them to repudiate their former profession for the same reason that they made it, namely, their worldly interest. And there would be some who, although sincere, would temporarily fail because they lack sufficient understanding and/or grace, as Peter did in his denial. On the other hand, there are many in the Christian Church who do believe its tenets with greater understanding and devotion. These, we would expect, would not deny these tenets although their lives were threatened, for their faith would include a knowledge and fellowship with God that is worth infinitely more than life. They would conclude that their present sufferings are not worthy to be compared with the glory which is yet to be revealed. They would be expected to embrace the sword, to smile at wild animals, to sing in the flames.

Now the historical record is a confirmation of what we would have expected. There have been Christians, to be sure, who have denied the faith to save their lives; there have been those who have been faithful to the death. The presence of recanters in the ranks of professed Christians proves nothing about the truth of the Christian religion, but only the falsity or weakness of their own profession. But the great question of this chapter is: what do martyrs prove about the truth of Christianity?

Negatively, the total absence of martyrs would probably prove Christianity false. That is to say, if Christianity had produced no persons who were faithful under trial, either it would not be the religion of God, or there would have been no true Christians. But if there were no true Christians in the Christian church, there could hardly be any anywhere. Therefore, without martyrs the Christian religion would be proved false; for if there were no martyrs, there could hardly be any true disciples, and if Christianity has produced no true disciples, it cannot be the religion of God.

Does someone demur at this last point, saying that it is too sweeping? Consider this: If the Christian religion is true, then this truth and the power of God which is in this truth would produce some adherents, as indeed it claims it will, in all generations. If, therefore, there is a persecution of the Christian religion, it is unthinkable that the genuine adherents would not be among those threatened. And if they were threatened, some of them would surely then exhibit under fire the trueness of their faith. But if there were no martyrs, no persons who proved their faith when it was tested by fire, there simply would be no Christians. This is the reason we say that if there had been no martyrs, this fact alone would have disproved the truth of the Christian religion.

The question now is, does the presence of martyrs prove the truth of Christianity? No, for as we have already said, men may sometimes die for something other than truth. But martyrdom surely confirms the truth of the faith. And there are various characteristics of Christian martyrs which augment the corroborative power of this argument.

First, there were multitudes of men and women who died for the Christian faith. The number of those who through the centuries have died out of loyalty to Jesus Christ can only be tabulated in the thousands of thousands. This phenomenon utterly amazed Napoleon and convinced him of the absolute superiority of the hold which the absent Christ still had over His followers, compared to the hold which the magnetic French general in person had over his.

Also, the invisibility of Christ accentuates the power of His Spirit. Christ Himself had said to those disciples who had been with Him in the days of His flesh that they were blessed in believing in Him but that, "Blessed are they that have not seen, and yet have believed" (John 20:29). Sometimes a leader by the sheer force of his personality is able to command loyalty to the death. But here is a person who, though absent from the flesh now for two thousand years, has as many men dying for Him today as died in the days of the Roman Empire when His memory was freshest. There is now no beat of marching drums, no fanfare, no spectacle, no vision; but Jesus still rules in the hearts of millions of persons. For His sake they count not their own lives dear.

Third, consider the types of persons who have been Christian martyrs. We have known of martyrs for other causes, but these have been rather rare personalities. Men who simply would not permit themselves to be dominated by any other, who would preserve their freedom rather than their life. There are persons like this, and they will die for what they hold dear. But Christian martyrs are not exceptional but commonplace people. There were great persons among them, but it was the rank and file who swelled the ranks of martyrs to the vast multitude which it has become. There has never been in the history of the world anything else even approximating this phenomenon. Never have so many ordinary people died for anything as have died for the honor of Jesus Christ.

Fourth, consider the sufferings of the martyrs. If there never has been another such a multitude as have died for the glory of Christ, neither have there ever been elsewhere such sufferings undergone in the course of martyrdom as the Christians have known. They have been torn apart by wild beasts; they have been covered with oil and pitch and burned alive to light arenas; they have been burned by slow fire before vast multitudes; they have had their tongues pulled out; they have been placed in solitary towers for years; they have been slowly drowned by rising tides; they have watched their children tortured and killed before their eyes; they have had holes drilled in their heads and filled with hot lead. There is nothing which the ingenuity of men or devils could contrive which has not been used to test the love of these men, women, and children for the name of Jesus Christ. Under any and all of these fiendish trials the martyrs have not only remained loyal, but have prayed and sung and rejoiced for the privilege of so dying.

This brings us to the fifth consideration—the spirit in which they died. For one thing, they died with a forgiving word on their lips. Torture usually brings out the worst spirit in the sufferer. He resents those who cause him such pain, and though he can do nothing by way of vengeance, he will at least retaliate with oaths and threats and curses. Christians, however, have not followed the ways of this world in dying any more than in living, but have followed in the footsteps of their Lord, who "when he suffered threatened not." Just as He forgave those who crucified Him, so His disciples have prayed for those who have persecuted them. From the first martyr Stephen on down through the centuries, the Christians have been wont to die blessing those who have put them to death and praying for those who have hated them. They have considered themselves blessed in being permitted to die for the Name and have wished that their persecutors could know the wonderful love of God. The Christian spirit has never been lovelier than when suffering. It has been like that spikenard which, when the vase in which it was carried was broken, filled all the room with its fragrance.

For another thing, their strength has been apparent. It is, after all, a dreadful ordeal to face death unnecessarily when it can be avoided by a mere abjuration. And when this death is accompanied with tortures, it becomes all the more difficult to face. But Christians have faced it; multitudes of all sorts of Christians have faced it. This has taken courage, very great courage indeed. Its sheer manliness leaves the world amazed. One martyr was afraid that he would be unable to face the flames. He tried to steel himself for the torment by holding his finger in the flame of a candle but could not endure even that. Yet when the time came for him to be burned alive, he went serenely and bravely to his death. Another martyr temporarily lost his courage and signed a recantation. Later he not only corrected his failure, but when he was burned, placed first in the fire the hand which had signed the recantation, holding it there until it was consumed.

Again they have been surprisingly joyful in these most unpropitious moments when the last thing to be expected would be joy. Perhaps they could be courageous, and perhaps they could even forgive, but how could they possibly be happy? Nevertheless, they have been happy and have died with joy in their hearts and songs on their lips. And this has often been the case. In Montpelier in southern France one can see an open park area where multitudes of men and women were put to death for their faith in Christ. One learns from history that when these people died, they sang Psalms as the fires rose about them. They sang so happily and so lustily that the authorities were obliged to hire a band to play music that would drown out their joyful songs of praise. Such is the spirit of the martyrs of Jesus Christ, for whom "to live is Christ and to die is gain."

Archibald Alexander, the nineteenth-century Princeton apologist, has well summarized the testimony of the martyrs, especially of those of the early church:

Persons of all ages, of all conditions of life, and of both sexes, exhibited under protracted and cruel torments, a fortitude, a patience, a meekness, a spirit of charity and forgiveness, a cheerfulness, yea often a triumphant joy, of which there are no examples to be found in the history of the world. They rejoiced when they were arrested; cheerfully bade adieu to their nearest and dearest relatives; gladly embraced the stake; welcomed the wild beasts let loose to devour them; smiled on the horrible apparatus by which their sinews were to be stretched, and their bones dislocated and broken; uttered no complaints; gave no indication of pain when their bodies were enveloped in flames; and when condemned to die, begged of their friends to interpose no obstacle to their felicity (for such they esteemed martyrdom), not even by prayer for their deliverance. What more than human fortitude was this? By what spirit were these despised and persecuted people sustained? What natural principles in the human constitution can satisfactorily account for such superiority to pain and death? Could attachment to an impostor inspire them with such feelings? No; it was the promised presence of the risen Jesus which upheld them, and filled them with assurance and joy.

PART IV

A CONSIDERATION OF SOME OBJECTIONS TO CHRISTIANITY

21

Objections from Evolution and Anthropology

SOME believe that evolution proves Christianity to be false. But whether it does or does not cannot be answered without a definition of evolution. If evolution had one and only one meaning it might not be too difficult to decide whether it is compatible with Christianity. But since it does not, there is no easy answer to the problem. For if the question is asked, "Is evolution compatible with Christianity?" another question immediately arises, "Which evolution?"

Some persons mean by evolution the doctrine that a process accounts for the existence of all things. "In the beginning Evolution said, 'Let there be light,' and there was light." This "causal evolution" or evolutionary process as the cause of all things is difficult to conceive and even more difficult to relate to other things such as Christianity. That is to say, when a person says that evolution brings all things into being, does he construe this creative evolution to be a static or a changing being? If it is an unchanging being, we remark, "Oh, you are calling God by the name of evolution!"

Evolution, in the sense of causal process, is not an explanation, but rather it needs an explanation. Either it exists in and of itself, or it depends on something else. Clearly, if it depends on something else, it cannot be the explanation of the other, but the other, of it. But can it exist in and of itself so as to be the explanation of other things? If it can and does, then it must be self-existent, intelligent, personal and moral as we have already shown. In that case it would not be evolution but the living personal God. So then evolution, in this causal sense, cannot be incompatible with theism or disprove it, for it would take theism to account for such an evolution.

Suppose we use the term "evolution" not in a causal but in a modal sense. That is, suppose we construe the word to signify the means by which things have come to be what they are. It is clear on the surface of it that this can pose no problem for theism. If evolution is modal or merely a means, it must be used by something or someone other than itself. No one can qualify for that role but God Himself. So once again, it would not be God that needs evolution, but evolution that needs God.

But does modal evolution conflict with Christianity? Theism itself may not involve any theory of the means by which the world has been developed by God, but Christianity does have something to say on the subject. Does what it says conflict with what nature reveals? Let us first of all ascertain just what the Bible does teach about the origin and preservation of the world, then what modal evolution teaches. After that we will be in a position to conclude whether they agree or conflict.

The Bible teaches several things about this world's origin and preservation. First, the world was brought into being by divine fiat, by the mere word of His power, out of nothing. "In the beginning God created the heavens and the earth" (Gen. 1:1). Second, the time during which God brought this world into being is not definite in the Bible. It is said to have been six "days," but the Bible does not always use that word to mean a period of twenty-four hours. Nor does the expression "morning and evening" necessarily specify such periods, for these are mentioned before the sun and the moon are created, as well as afterward. Third, the Genesis account presents creation as proceeding on an ascending scale of complexity. That is, more advanced and complicated creatures are made later than the simpler. Specifically, the higher mammals and man are not created until the sixth day. Fourth, reproduction of different groups is to be each "after its own kind." This expression is not further defined so that the reader cannot know what the precise reference is, whether to kingdom, family, class, genus, order, species, or variety. Fifth, man is specially created; at least, his soul is. God gave to him a quality not given to the other beings made. He breathed on him and he became a "living soul." He said, "Let us make man in our own image."

Let us see whether or not modal evolution is compatible with this account of Biblical creation. On the first point (that a personal God created all things *ex nihilo*) there is no problem, because modal evolution has nothing to say about ultimate origins. On the second point, which maintains that no definite time of creation is mentioned in the Bible, there is no necessary conflict. Theories of modal evolution usually call for a very long period of time, but there is no necessary proof that the Biblical indefiniteness on this point is not capable of accommodating scientific theories. With respect to the time associated with man's appearance in the creation, some possibility of conflict emerges, though not precisely with modal evolution so much as with anthropology. That is, modal evolution as such does not date the arrival of man, but anthropological researchers may or may not date him. Some do, and they usually date him very early. Is it earlier than the Bible dates him? This subject, since it pertains to anthropology proper rather than evolution in general, we will discuss later in the chapter.

Third, the ascending complexity of the creation as presented in Genesis chapter one and the date of modal evolution are conspicuously corroborative. But the fourth point, concerned with the reproduction of each "after its kind," brings up a crucial comparison with modal evolution. Now there is a possible conflict, depending on our conception of modal evolution. That is, if we think of modal evolution as Charles Darwin thought of it, as the development of all things from original gemmules or cells through a continuous progress from within (apart from further creation) to the highest degree of complex existence, we have a manifest divergence from the Biblical view of things. If, however, evolution is conceived of as less comprehensive and more restricted in compass, there is no necessary conflict. If an evolutionist holds to the multiple origins theory, as many do, and thinks of variations taking place within these broad frameworks which were "given" or "there" and possibly created by God, then the flexibility and indefiniteness of "after its kind" does not preclude the possibility of such an evolution. There may be some question whether the "multiple origins" view can be proven, but there is no question that the comprehensive Darwinian theory has never begun to be proven. There is a question as to whether it should be considered an hypothesis, but certainly it is not a theory, much less a fact. So we may conclude that no proven fact of science is at any necessary variance with the Bible on this fourth point.

The fifth point is extremely important, of course. Genesis represents man as specially created in that he was made in the divine image by a breath or special fiat of God. Does modal evolution teach otherwise? No modal evolutionist, as an evolutionist or as a biologist, teaches or can teach otherwise.

That is because this question lies out of his domain. It does not come within his scope as a biologist. If he comments on it, he is speaking as a psychologist or philosopher but not as a biologist or anthropologist. No amount of biological observation can possibly discover a soul. Nor can any evolutionist find evidence for or against its transmission from one form to another. If a man concludes that the soul is not what it is defined to be, not something different from the physical organism but rather a function or aspect of the body, he must arrive at that conclusion as a philosopher or psychologist but not as a biologist. And the soundness of his view has to be defended or attacked on the same grounds. Since we have already written enough to show, we think, that such a view of the soul is unsound, we need not here rehearse the evidence. We conclude, therefore, that the biologist or evolutionist as such cannot differ with Genesis on this point.

But let us now face more specifically the anthropological problem. Do we find, in the researches of men in this field, discoveries which conflict with the Biblical view of man? It is thought by some scientists and theologians that we do. It is maintained that the antiquity of man in geology and anthropology is far greater than the Bible allows. Is this the case? Let us see what are the findings of science, then what is the teaching of Scripture.

There are several observations to be made about the findings of science on this subject. First, it seems difficult to say that there are "findings" in any conclusive sense of that word. That is, certain and settled evidence about the antiquity of prehistoric man does not seem to exist. Many remains of manlike creatures have been found. But there is the greatest diversity of opinion among the experts in almost every case. One anthropologist is of the opinion that such and such a group of bones shows the presence of a true man; another is dubious about the same collection of bones. We do not want to say with Chesterton that scientists with their bones are about as bad as dogs with theirs, but there does seem to be lacking anything like a consensus about these fossils. There have even been proven hoaxes. One writer observes that the series of pictorial sketches of men ascending from lower forms which used to be displayed so conspicuously, and apparently so demonstratively, in elementary science books, appear less and less conspicuously and seem to be considered less and less demonstrative as the years go on. There has been a notable devolution of evolutionary series since the days of the admittedly fraudulent Ernst Haeckel, who justified himself on the grounds, he said, that everyone else was doing the same thing.

We do not wish to be, or appear to be, obscurantist. We do not question the science of geology or of anthropology. We have keen admiration for specialists who from a few remains are able to make remarkable reconstructions of entire skeletons with amazing accuracy in many cases. We certainly do not wish to bring any opprobrium on any science because there have been some rash mistakes made by some of its investigators. Nor do we wish to deny that a man can be a competent scientist although he has made a blunder at one time or another. On the other hand, we freely admit the errors of theologians and their capacity for error. All we are attempting to say here is what hundreds of scientists have said themselves, that science is no sacred cow, that it is not infallible, and specifically that the limitations upon all branches of learning apply to this anthropological area also, so that it can hardly be said that the date of the beginnings of prehistoric man is established as a demonstrated and indisputable fact. It seems to us that the most that can be said is that we do have some remains of prehistoric man, but that none of these remains are capable of precise dating as yet, although some things may be fairly accurately estimated by various modern methods. It looks probable to a number of specialists that genuine human remains go back from thirty to a hundred thousand years, but this seems only highly probable even to these men.

Now let us consider the Bible's teaching concerning the antiquity of man. First, the earliest, rather certain date is that of Abraham, about 1800 B.C. Second, for the dates of the events before Abraham and Genesis 11, we have no clues from the Bible except the genealogies. Third, we know that the Biblical genealogies do not purport to be exhaustive of every person in every line. This can be shown by a comparison of some of the genealogies of Genesis with parallel ones in the New Testament concerning the ancestry of Christ. Furthermore, we have no idea how many individuals, or families for that matter, may be deleted from the genealogies of Genesis. (It should be said in all fairness, on the other hand, that we do not know from the Bible that these genealogies are not almost complete.) Fourth, as indicated above, it cannot be demonstrated beyond all doubt that the days of Genesis are twenty-four hours in duration. We know of some who believe that they are and who present a very cogent series of considerations. But we know of no one who thinks that his argumentation is sufficiently conclusive that he dare become dogmatic about it. The general consensus seems to favor the notion that the days could have been and were eras. We include this point because in a very general sense it seems relevant, but actually it is hardly so. It bears only on the question of how long God took to bring man into being, not on the question of his antiquity or how long he has been on earth. That is, the days of Genesis may be as long as you please, but still the created Adam was a historical figure whose history merges with the genealogies of Genesis.

We may come, therefore, to this conclusion concerning the teaching of the Bible about the antiquity of man. Because of uncertainty about genealogies, we cannot fix certain limits for the antiquity of man, although it probably must be said that the Bible does not want to represent the antiquity of man as very great.

Putting the two pictures together, that of science and the Bible, what do we see? We see no necessary conflict for the simplest reason that neither science nor Genesis present fixed dates. Each set of approximate dates is very vague and uncertain. About all that can be said is that anthropologists tend to date genuine man earlier than the Bible tends to date Adam and his descendants. But until more definite evidence from one side or the other is in, it seems wise to let the matter rest.

22

Objections from Determinism

A FUNDAMENTAL objection to Christianity, and in fact to all religion, is drawn from determinism. The conviction is often expressed that we think what we think because we are taught what we are taught. If we were taught differently we would think and believe differently. For example, some persons are Christians because their parents taught them to be Christians and other people are Muslims because their parents taught them to be Muslims. Some are not religious at all because their parents taught them not to be religious, or more accurately taught them to be nonreligious. The "truth" of religion, therefore, is hardly a meaningful question. The truth is whatever one has been taught is the truth. It is as simple as that.

Now this criticism, although it is made frequently and many seem to think that it has cogency, cannot be taken seriously if it is to be taken seriously. That is, if it is so that we are what we have been taught, then we must conclude that the person who says that we are what we have been taught says so because he has been so taught. We simply can not take seriously the criticism that all truth is merely what any given person has been taught to consider true without applying that formula to the statement itself, and that immediately destroys it. Consequently, if we give any consideration whatever to this statement, we thereby assume that it is something more than what the maintainer has been taught. But that too destroys the statement. And so the deterministic criticism is fundamentally self-destructive.

Really, evolution as a problem is but a phase of the general problem of determinism. It explains the origin of the species including me and therefore tends to explain who I am and how and why I act as I do. Sociological determinism only carries the matter a step further. It studies the pattern which immediately bears on my life and by that means tries to explain why I do as I do and think as I think. Evolution, in other words, gives my broad background, while sociology gives my more immediate background. Each is ultimately an attempt to explain me.

All scientific disciplines are useful, and the more that I know about me the better I should be able to live. We have no quarrel with, but only appreciation for these various efforts at learning more about man. The only point at which we raise any protest is when someone says that by a knowledge of backgrounds we can completely explain how man acts as he does, since we know that he acts as he does because he has precisely the background which he has. As we have already shown, this simply cannot be because if it were so, its being so would destroy the truth of the very statement itself. For example, L. A. Feuerbach has written, *"Der Mensch ist was er isst."* ("Man is what he eats"). The trouble with that statement is that the man who wrote it must be what he eats as well as the man who reads it. If I read the statement and thereafter conclude that I am what I eat, I am being rather foolish. I am foolish because I have taken the author seriously but have forgotten that by taking him seriously I destroy him. For if I take him seriously, that is to say, if I believe his thesis that "man is what he eats," then I admit that the author of that thesis is what he eats. But if that is the case, then some of his ideas may have been the product of the spinach he had for supper, and the things he wrote in chapter twelve may have been produced by pie a la mode. And the conclusion of all his volumes may have come right out of a can of beans; or, more likely, directly from a roll of baloney. We should be wondering what the books would have been like if the author had eaten the spinach on Thursday instead of on Friday and how different the conclusion would have been if it had followed a banana split rather than the beans. Moreover, it is conceivable that if Feuerbach had had some smoked herring, he might have concluded that man is not what he eats. There is one thing that we dare not do with such an author, and that is take him seriously. If man is what he eats, then he is not what he eats. If he is not what he eats, then there is some possibility that food, whatever influence it may have upon him, does not altogether determine what he is.

Another area in which determinism raises its head is the area of interpretation. "That is your interpretation," it is often said, and with a sense of finality that is meant to show that the interpretation is therefore not valid for the protestor. "That is your interpretation" is apparently intended to carry with it the implication that our interpretations necessarily differ, as much as to say, "You have your interpretation and I have mine." Now it is true that you may have your interpretation and I may have mine, but it does not follow that your interpretation is valid for you and not for me, nor that mine is not valid for you but only for me. The mere statement "that's your interpretation" says nothing at all except that that is your interpretation. It may, as far as those words are concerned, be the correct interpretation. And if it is the correct interpretation, it ought to be mine also. And if my interpretation is the correct one, it ought to be yours also. There is no reason for thinking of interpretations as we think of hats. "That is my hat" does carry with it the implication that it is not yours because it is mine. We do not share hats. But interpretations are not hats. They should be shared. If I interpret something in a particular way, it should be because I think that is the correct interpretation. I should then seek to persuade you of the correctness of it so that it may become your interpretation too. In other words, I try to prove that a hat is mine to demonstrate private property. But I try to prove that an interpretation is mine to prove common property. Interpretation is the intellectual coin of the mental realm.

After all, interpreting is inevitable. If one interpretation sets us off from all others precisely because it is our own, then this inevitable activity would be the most divisive activity conceivable. But what reason have we for saying that one interpretation sets us off from others? None whatsoever, except the old deterministic assumption. We are once again assuming that your thinking and your interpreting must necessarily be different from mine because it is yours and you are what you were born, where you live, what you eat, et cetera. But we have shown again and again the futility of this position. If an interpretation is yours because of what you eat, then it has no validity for anyone including yourself. In other words, if it is only your interpretation, it is not even your interpretation. Hence the formula is utterly invalid and must be ruled out of serious discourse, and once again we are thrown back on the healthy mental activity of ascertaining which interpretation is correct. If your interpretation is different from mine, you should not say, "That is your interpretation"; but, "Your interpretation is incorrect at such and such a point," and then proceed to show me my error. If you convince me, I should accept your interpretation and correct mine accordingly. If my interpretation differs from yours I should not be willing to leave the matter there. Rather I should show you how I have come to my conclusion, indicate why I have not come to yours and why you should not retain it. If my reasoning is cogent, you should acknowledge it and change your previously held opinions accordingly.

We suppose that everyone grants the truth of what has been said above. But you may be thinking that men simply do not act that way. W. G. T. Shedd has a sermon title which is very apropos here: "The approbation of the good is not the love of it." That is, persons often approve of what is right but, not loving it, do not do it. This is the noetic influence of sin or the effect of evil on the mind of man. It is granted that men often corrupt their thinking by their prejudices and seek to justify their errors for some ulterior motive. Frequently they are even unwilling to listen to a divergent view because they refuse to entertain its unacceptable implications. But these things should not be. Error is not innocent and every idle thought will be brought into the judgment. We must give heed to ourselves how we think. We shall have our interpretations, indeed, but they must be sound interpretations. Precisely for this reason there must be free intellectual intercourse among men, candid discussion of different positions, and complete candor in seeking truth.

It is admittedly true that each man is a private person and he sees things as he sees them. But the eye and the mind and all the faculties are made on the same pattern in all persons. There is, after all, a common sphere of understanding, and there is a possibility of communication. This communication would not be possible if each person were sealed off by his individuality from every other person. The particular background which each person admittedly has, may be taken account of when he is communicating with another person.

Otherwise there would be no possibility of intercommunication. In other words, we may adjust our thinking to grasp the meaning of the other person. But assuming that we do this, we admit the possibility of our understanding the other person.

It is sometimes assumed that each person necessarily distorts information as it comes through his mind. A person may indeed distort it, but he need not. Furthermore, he can discover or be shown that he has distorted it. Indeed there would be no meaning to the very word "distort" unless knowledge could be accurately apprehended.

While men may distort knowledge, they need not do so. It is wrong to think that man is like water which by its very nature distorts the light which passes through it, giving a misleading image. To be more accurate we should say that man is like water when he does, because of prejudice of one kind or another, distort the knowledge which comes to him; but he can, if he will, not distort.

There would seem to be nothing in the nature of man as such which makes it inevitable for him to distort knowledge, rendering his interpretations necessarily private rather than public. One man's mind, being made on a common pattern, would be capable of seeing things as any other mind sees them. If he does make a mistake, his mind, made on the same pattern as other minds, would be capable of receiving correction from these other minds. His background could cause him to read things into some knowledge which do not properly belong there. But another mind could understand what he had done and point it out, and he would be capable of understanding the correction and making it.

We repeat, by way of conclusion, that if it is not true that man can understand objectively and correct in accordance with objectivity, then there is no possibility of knowledge at all. As we have said, when someone says, "That's your interpretation," he is necessarily assuming objectivity. We need not go over this ground again. But it does need to be repeated that there is no reason for thinking that our thoughts are determined irrespective of ourselves, making objectivity impossible. Or if they are, then we must face the dismal fact that we cannot predicate anything, dare not open our mouths, cannot even be subjective, can know nothing whatsoever— not even that we know nothing whatsoever.

It may well be a criticism of this volume that it devotes so much space to the problem of determinism. My explanation, if not justification, is that after many addresses on college campuses and especially after many private conferences with college students, I have been impressed with the prevalence of this vein of thinking and the formidable obstacle it raises for all who seem interested in faith. For example, I can well remember spending a week on a certain Christian college campus and having hundreds of conversations with men and women concerning Christianity. These collegians had their problems, and they were problems of all varieties. But the thing which impressed me most of all was the prevalence of the deterministic problem. It quite outweighed problems in all other areas. There were at least twice as many students exercised about difficulties in this area as in the field of the physical sciences, for example. They were far more perturbed about a sociological or psychological determinism than about evolution, anthropology, Biblical criticism, or even personal morality. Indeed this problem penetrated all these other areas, for when difficulties arose in the other areas, it was often this underlying determinism that seemed to haunt the student.

But one last matter before we leave the problem of determinism. Some grant all that has been said in this chapter but still come back with more. They say, "Very well, everything is determined including my statement that everything is determined. Suppose that I admit that. I will also admit that I may have to think differently of things than I have previously; but if it is true, it is true—let the consequences be what they will. Here I stand!"

What shall we say to this fatalist who is fatalistic about his fatalism? We fear that we have not made the significance of our argument clear to him as yet. He seems to think that so long as he simply admits that fatalism is true, he can go on with the business of living as usual. He will, he thinks, simply recognize that he too is determined and let the matter rest at that. But what we have tried to say is that he cannot let the matter rest at that. His is a position of no rest, of nonequilibrium. He cannot rest in it. He must go one way or another, but he cannot stand there. But what do we mean by this?

When we say that a determinist cannot admit his determinism and let it go at that, we mean that he cannot even affirm his determinism. To affirm determinism or fatalism is to make what one professes to be a true judgment of fact. But as we have tried to say *ad nauseam,* if this determinism is true, then the statement that determinism is true cannot be true. It cannot be true because it is a determined statement that has no correspondence to objective, but only to subjective reality. It, therefore, cannot be true. And if it is not true, the determinist cannot say that it is. He cannot say, "This is true, and now since I know that all truth is subjective and does not correspond to reality, I shall say no more." He cannot say even that much. He should, of course, be silent ever after if determinism is true, but he cannot be vocal long enough to say that it is true.

As a matter of fact, determinists are as vocal before and after they declare their determinism as others are. But the point is that they have no right to predication. It is meaningless. And if they predicate anyway and then say that they will take the consequences of their predication, they should not only thereafter hold their peace forever (which they do not do), but they should not have spoken in the first place. They can only speak on nondeterministic suppositions. They must needs be nondeterminists long enough to declare their determinism, just as they would have to rely on God long enough to declare that there is no God. If this is not patently impossible, we do not know what is. And if it is not clear to all that a person holding such a position ought to be silent, not only in his speech, but in his very thought, then we do not know how it can be made clear. If the determinist will insist on speaking, we shall, I am afraid, have politely to disregard him until he returns to the canons of rationality, must we not?

23

Objections from Biblical Criticism

CRITICISM of the integrity and infallibility of the Bible is often made. A recent work says that verbal inspiration is an "almost blasphemous error." Another writer is of the same opinion: "Idolators of the letter of the Bible must be converted to true worshipers of the spirit of the Bible. Only then will the prestige of the divine book be saved." Still another speaks of "the incredible fatuity on the part of the literalist, who insists on the 'absolute inerrance' of Scripture!" One writer finds the literalist more than fatuous, saying that "literal infallibility of Scripture, held to its last logic, would risk a trip to the insane asylum." A certain pastor thinks that the Bible as it stands is the source of the crime wave; it must be censored and expurgated. Many learned and popular writers find Eden a delightful myth, and one of them warns about making various Bible stories into anything more than that:

I can no more understand that any serious injury can come to my moral nature from disbelieving Samson than from disbelieving in Jack the Giant-Killer. I care as little for Goliath as for the giant Blunderbore. I am glad that children should amuse themselves with nursery stories, but it is shocking that they should be ordered to believe in them as solid facts, and then be told that such superstition is essential to morality.

However, the Bible regards itself as inspired. Christ clearly claimed inspiration for the Old Testament and promised it for the New Testament, as we have indicated. It was concerning the Old Testament that He said not a jot nor a tittle should pass away until all be fulfilled. "Scripture," He said, "cannot be broken." In exegetical argument with the Pharisees He makes His point rest on a single word. Indeed, the case is so conclusive that radical scholars, such as Jülicher, who themselves do not accept the doctrine, admit that the orthodox are right in claiming that Christ taught it. J. B. Green has observed that the Bible asserts its own inspiration some three thousand times.

The historic doctrine of the Church as well as the teaching of the Bible is the inerrancy of Scripture. Well and good. But in the last two centuries there has been a great revolt. What will the outcome be? We believe it will be victory for the historic doctrine. And, furthermore, we believe that the justification of the historic doctrine of inspiration is now in process. The first step in this process is the stronger and stronger establishment of the integrity and reliability of the text of Scripture. Meek, of Toronto, writing in *Religious Education* on the trend of Old Testament scholarship during the preceding ten years, found the outstanding characteristic to be the growing esteem for the Massoretic or Hebrew text. Whereas at the beginning of the century as we have mentioned in the Introduction, the first thing that a critic would do was to amend the text to fit his theory, now that is about the last thing which he dares to do. Orlinsky, in *Religious Education*, July-August, 1952, shows the same high regard for the Massoretic text. In 1951, Thiele put out a work entitled *The Mysterious Numbers of the Hebrew*

Kings, which Old Testament specialists think is a significant book. One of its incidental conclusions concerns the accuracy of the Biblical text. Thiele never found Josephus more reliable than the Bible. It certainly cannot be said that Wellhausenism is dead as long as some foremost Old Testament experts are still committed to it. There is no doubt, however, that this theory is on its way out as any number of scholars indicate. S. W. Baron, for example, in his *A Social and Religious History of the Jews* (two volumes), while still holding to the documentary hypothesis, speaks of Wellhausenism as having ruled until 1937. Then too it is significant that scholars such as Albright, Alt, Allis, and a host of others have turned from the hypothesis of the evolutionary development of Old Testament religion. There are more and more men impressed by what James Orr, J. B. Green, and others were saying half a century ago. In this connection, Albright's review of Allis' *Five Books of Moses,* is interesting. About the only serious criticism which the great Johns Hopkins archaeologist offered to the former Westminster Seminary professor was that he had not quoted more recent works to establish his thesis that Moses wrote or could have written the Pentateuch. We have often wondered, since reading that review, what Allis would say about the criticism. There is no doubt that Allis has read Orelli and the others whom Albright suggested. We rather suppose the reason he did not quote more of them was that the point had been established so long ago that there was no reason for giving the credit to later men, simply because they were more liberal and therefore more likely to be listened to.

Basically, the same development has taken place in the New Testament field. Strauss had questioned the reliability of the evangelists and had tried to find the hand of the second-century church behind the Gospel narratives, especially the portions which entertained a high view of Christ. Others followed him and became especially convinced of his theory in the case of the Gospel according to John. It was so emphatically "theological" that it was utterly taken for granted that an eyewitness like the apostle John could not have written it. It had to have been written late in the second century at the earliest. Then came the discovery of the Rylands manuscript with the earliest fragment of any portion of the New Testament ever found. It was dated, at the latest the middle of the second century, at the earliest the first quarter of the second century. And what should it be but a portion of the Gospel of John. In 1952 a new edition of Loisy's *Origins of the New Testament* was issued. In it the radical French scholar had blandly assumed, along with all other radical and liberal scholars of his time, the late date of John. The reviewer for *Interpretation*, therefore, has this remark to make: "It would perhaps have been kind not to publish the translation of A. F. Loisy's *Origins of the New Testament.* Positions, such as the date of the Fourth Gospel, which were speculative possibilities at the time of writing, have since been contradicted by direct evidence." We demur at the phrase "speculative possibilities," for they were really speculative prejudices, based on a reluctance to admit that the high view of Jesus entertained in John could possibly have been true to the facts. Meanwhile, other scholars were examining other Gospels and finding that the high view of Christ was ubiquitous. Wrede, after working over the Second Gospel, cried, "Mark is as bad as John." He meant Mark was as good as John, for he had as high a Christology. Someone has said that since Schweitzer's *Quest of the Historical Jesus,* no first-rate scholar has dared to write a life of Jesus viewing Him as a mere reformer without high theological overtones.

So there has been a growing distrust of the so-called *Form-geschicte* school. Their attempts to get back of the writer to an unseen hand are being regarded more and more as futile.

One German critic has remarked that these men act as if they could see the grass grow. It would take that kind of acumen to penetrate as these men profess to be able to do. They are ever finding tendencies here and there. Hence the term *Tendenzkritik*. The trouble is, as Moore observed in his *History of Christian Thought*, "the Tendenzkritik had its own tendencies." The eminent New Testament conservative Ned Stonehouse has soberly observed, "No really objective criterion, not excluding the criterion advanced by form-criticism, has been discovered whereby one may remove the supposedly unhistorical accretions of tradition and get back to an original historical stratum of solid fact."

The third justification is the vindication of Biblical accuracy in the little details. That rabbit which did not seem to meet the Mosaic description and which was such a stumbling block to Karl Barth's acceptance of verbal inspiration is not too difficult to explain, as Barth's interrogators showed. It has been shown that the hare does chew its food the second time as the Bible says, even though it does not have the characteristic four-chambered stomach of the typical ruminant. Then too, the quails of Exodus have found their way into court. Harry Rimmer was challenged by an American newspaper which maintained that if the Exodus story is true, there would have been enough quail piled up over the countryside that each of the six million Israelites would have had about 69,629 per meal. But Rimmer pointed out that the Bible does not say the Israelites ate all that fell. Nor does the record say that the quail were piled up two cubits high but rather that they were in reach at that height. Furthermore, we appear to be dealing with a miracle. The court awarded the case to Rimmer. Noldeke and other scholars were perfectly confident not long ago that Gen. 14 was impossible. The journey of the Eastern Kings whom Abraham pursued was impossible because their names were unheard of, the route was unknown, and the travel was much too much for that day. Every one of these points has been refuted now. At one time, just about every liberal scholar was absolutely certain that Moses could not have been the author of the Pentateuch because writing was not known at that time. Liberals today do not like to be reminded of that. The numerous mistakes of the author of Acts have been shown, one by one, to be the mistakes of the critic rather than the author. Most of the so-called scientific errors of the Bible have been traced to the changeability of scientific hypothesis or the popular, nontechnical character of Biblical language. In the former category, A. T. Pierson notes that of the eighty-two theories which the French Institute considered hostile to the Bible in 1800, not one now stands. In the latter category, A. H. Strong observes that if the Bible were to use technical rather than popular phraseology, instead of saying, "At sunset, Isaac went out to meditate," it would read, "When the rotation of the earth on its axis was such that the rays from the solar luminary impinged horizontally on the retina, Isaac went out to meditate." And so it goes.

Over against all these random, and often irresponsible attacks we have the sober testimony of those who have studied the Bible long and hard. Dean Farrar said, "The widest range of learning and the acutest ingenuity of criticism has never discovered one single demonstrable error of fact or doctrine in the Old or New Testament." The massive scholar Strong wrote, "It may be safely said that science has not yet shown any fairly interpreted passage of Scripture to be untrue." The old anvil is still wearing out the hammers.

A fourth justification is seen in the awfulness of the alternatives to inerrancy. Strauss, in a sense, represented the apex of this revolt. And, in another sense, he showed how it would end. In 1835, in his *Leben Jesu*, he was showing us how to distrust the evangelists; and in 1874, in his *Der neue und der alte Glaube,* he had learned to distrust the evangel itself as he sank into materialism and despair. Again, if Christ could make a mistake at one point, why not at another? If we cannot trust Him when He speaks of Jonah or Sodom or Lot's wife, why can we trust Him when He speaks of the Kingdom of God, the ransom for sin, or His own Messiahship? Paine was frank enough when he said that we cannot believe Jesus when He said He is the Son of God. And Schenkel lays the ax at the root of the whole tree with these penetrating words: "If error is admitted at one point, it is admissible at all points."

A fifth justification, a corollary of the fourth, is the logic or consistency of the infallibilist position. After all, if the Bible is God's Word, it must be God's Word. We are reminded of the oft-quoted words, "Let God be God." Well then, "Let God's Word be God's Word." If God had something to say about astronomy, geology, history, arithmetic, politics, et cetera, He must be infallible there as well as in the area of religion. Granted that the Bible is not a textbook of this or that; still, if it is God's Word, it must be reliable on whatever it speaks. The author of this book is no scientist, philosopher, or economist. But if he makes bold to remark on any of these three, it is because he believes his remarks, however limited, to be strictly true. He does not feel at liberty to tell the truth in Church History, but to be irresponsible in every other area. God, of course, knows everything, and that makes it all the more certain that He would be accurate in secular matters as well as sacred ones. One thing is certain. If the whole Bible is not the inerrant Word of God, no one has ever devised, or ever can devise a way of telling where truth begins and falsehood leaves off.

Justification of the historic doctrine of inerrancy is in process. Justification is in process, and we expect the coming century to establish the trustworthiness of the Bible as the council of Nicaea established the deity of Christ. Since Nicaea, there has never been any question that the deity of Christ is the orthodox doctrine of the Christian Church. Men here and there have denied it, but it is patent to all that in so doing they are deviating from the historic Christian witness. So, we believe, the Biblical and historical doctrine of inerrancy will become established so firmly after the revolt of the past two centuries has passed, that no one will again question what is the historic position of the Christian Church concerning the Holy Scriptures of God.

The amazing Dead Sea Scrolls are already recognized as the greatest archaeological discovery of this century, even though the specialists in this field have not begun to decipher all of the finds. They are quite hesitant to commit themselves about the full significance of what has been discovered. Some of what has been said is being controverted by the experts. Far be it from us to pretend to any important knowledge in this area. Still it does not seem premature to say, and there seems already to be some consensus on this fact, that the upshot of the whole matter thus far is the further establishment of the prestige of the Bible, historically speaking.

We do not know what the future holds, but on the basis of what is known, we can reasonably anticipate that the Word of God will continue to shine ever brighter until the perfect day.

24

Objections from the Shortcomings
of the Church

PROBABLY the greatest arguments for and the greatest arguments against Christianity are Christians. Noble Christians, especially martyrs, are living syllogisms:

> My life has divinity about it;
> This divinity did not come from me;
> Therefore, it derives from Christ who lives within me.

On the other hand, merely nominal or hypocritical Christians are also living syllogisms:

> My life is an ignoble thing;
> But I profess that Christ is my guide;
> Therefore, on my profession, Christ must lead
> into ignobility and be ignoble.

The major faults which the world finds with professing Christians are three in number. First, it finds fault with some members as they are in themselves, hypocritical. Second, it finds fault with Christians in relation to one another, denominational. Third, it finds fault with Christians in relation to those outside the Church, "holier-than-thou."

First, the world finds fault with some Christians, charging them with being hypocrites. They say that they will not believe in Christianity nor join the Church because there are so many hypocrites in it. Furthermore, they say, not only are there many unworthy persons in the Church, but there are many worthy ones outside it. If there are hypocrites in the Church, there are "pleasing pagans" in the world.

Now there is much here which the Church must confess. She cannot deny that there are hypocrites in her communion. Neither can she deny that some of them she should have kept out in the first place, had she been diligent about her Lord's business. And there are many that she could have removed, had she been sufficiently concerned for the honor of Jesus Christ, which she professes to desire more than all else. Furthermore, she must confess that the presence of hypocrites is a cogent argument against her. The world may be expected to judge the value of the Church from the products of her evangelism, and if these are the products, her cause does not look good. And the Church cannot contest the fact that there are many outside her communion who seem to be more Christian than many inside it. She must also grant that if the world is producing better persons than the Church, there is prima-facie evidence that the Church has lost its savor and is henceforth good for nothing but to be "cast out and trodden under foot of men."

In spite of all this, there are many things which may be said in reply to this serious criticism. First, it is far easier to call a person hypocrite than to prove him one. Human justice in any area is a very inadequate device for dealing with offenders. There are many underworld figures in the nation who are probably guilty of many things that should expose them to the penalties of law, yet it cannot be demonstrated that they are guilty. So it may be with persons in churches.

Also, there are many persons who will condemn the government for not prosecuting certain criminals, but the government would prosecute if it could get witnesses against them. Now the very critics may be witnesses who, nevertheless, refuse to testify. So with respect to the Church, some of those who condemn her for harboring hypocrites will not testify against them if they are brought to trial, but will continue to condemn the Church for not bringing them to trial and excommunication. And in other cases, there are persons who are "known" by all to be offenders but whom none can prove to be such.

Second, what is sometimes called harboring hypocrites is but throwing a cloak of charity over a son. That is to say, Christianity is a religion of gentleness and love, and it tries always to put the best possible construction on anyone's deeds. It would be slow to anger, believe all things, hope all things, endure all things. It regards all members as its children and is loathe to believe otherwise. It will come most reluctantly to the conclusion that any who profess Christ are reprobates. The Church acts toward her erring sons as David did toward Absalom for whom he wept, even though that son heaped every conceivable ignominy upon his affectionate father. It was the spirit of Joab that condemned David for his long-sufferings not the spirit of a father.

Third, the claim that there is an abundance of hypocrites in the Church is probably exaggerated. We suspect that so much is made of them because they stand out so conspicuously. This may very well be a backhanded compliment to the Church. We suppose that if the Church were actually overrun with false pretenders, the world would simply dismiss her from consideration rather than taking the trouble to level such a charge against her. This situation may be analogous to the well-known psychological experiment in which a class is shown a large piece of white paper imprinted with a single black dot. When the class is asked what it sees, the answer is the black dot. So it may be that the world sees the black dot in the Church rather than the much larger but, precisely for that reason, less conspicuous white mass.

Fourth, hypocrisy itself is, in one sense, an argument for truth. Someone has said that "hypocrisy is the tribute which vice pays to virtue." That is, the very fact that some persons take the trouble and run the risk of being hypocrites suggests that what they simulate is worthwhile. It is so good that a person will pretend to have it if he is actually lacking it. People do not make a career of feigning vice. There is nothing so commendable about vice that men will merely pretend to be vicious. As a matter of fact, they will pretend not to be when actually they are. Thus hypocrisy reveals the desirableness of good and the undesirableness of evil. In this case, it constitutes an oblique argument for Christianity.

Fifth, something may be said with respect to the "pleasing pagans" outside the Church. For one thing, "pleasingness" may be of no particular value. It may have reference, and usually does, to nothing but personal charm, wittiness, and other such qualities which, though they may be interesting, are not necessarily useful. When the real needs of life come, witticisms and the like are of little or no use, if they do not actually gall.

Furthermore, pagans are often so pleasing largely because they have nothing much to test their patience or their virtue. The world may be their oyster. They may be born with silver spoons in their mouths and have so many of the gifts of this world that their charm reflects no great credit on them. They may have a naturally good disposition, be normally healthy and spirited, and have good smart minds that make it easy for them to be the life of the party. We would not detract from these gifts. We simply note that it may not reflect any credit to the person's character but merely to his good fortune that he has them. In other words, it is not necessarily any favorable reflection on the effect of his philosophy or ethic that he is so-and-so but merely an indication of the kindness of providence toward him.

On the other hand, a far less charming person may be a far more virtuous person who does credit to the Christian religion. C. S. Lewis tells of a mythical Annie Bates who was naturally of an acid disposition but whom Christianity had greatly helped. Dick Firkin was naturally pleasing without any particular credit to himself. So in the end when the tally is struck, the Church will have accomplished more in what she has done for Annie Bates, than the world in what it has done for Dick Firkin. A product must be judged by the material from which it was made. The tendency of Christianity is to produce Christlike character, though that character may not emerge from an unlovely personality to be as conspicuously pleasing as that of another who has always been naturally attractive. Still there is more credit for Christianity than for its competitor in the case. One man may be a better athlete naturally than another man is after much skillful coaching. But no one will deny that that coach deserves more credit who makes a poor athlete into a good one, than the coach who makes a good athlete into a slightly better one.

Another thing which must be kept in mind when we are thinking of pleasing pagans is that the things which make them pleasing may be liabilities. Many men succumb easily to flattery, and many a person has had popular success because he has had no scruples to prevent him from indulging promiscuously in fulsome flattery. He is not a true friend, though he may be popular. On the other hand, sternness may not be popular with many people, but it may bring them closer to the truth. The stern man may be the best friend.

The world also finds fault with the Church in its internal

relations, that is, its denominationalism. It is argued that Christians do not love one another but rival and divide from one another sometimes out of actual hatred. Furthermore, how could these churches have *the* truth of God and be so diverse in their understanding of it? Are there not several hundred different denominations in the United States alone?

This again is a partly valid criticism. The existence of different denominations, especially so many of them, argues one of two things: either the Bible on which they are ostensibly based is not one but many and therefore not the Word of the one God, or there is something fundamentally wrong with the churches. We cannot entertain the first alternative if the Bible is the Word of God. We are, therefore, reluctantly driven to acknowledge that there is some serious fault in the churches themselves.

But having acknowledged so much, we press on to evaluate the significance of this disunion. What does the lamentable fact prove? Actually it proves the very thing which the Bible everywhere teaches, namely, that Christian people have much remaining corruption. Oddly enough, if the Church were perfect and enjoyed that degree of harmony which she should enjoy, the Bible would be proved in error. Such perfection and harmony would actually be an argument against, not for, Christianity.

But the Bible teaches that the best of Christians fall far short of the excellency of the character of Christ. Thus Paul counted himself not to have attained. John said that if we say we have no sin, we deceive ourselves and the truth is not in us. Christ taught His disciples to pray regularly, "Forgive us our debts." Some are "weak" and must be received "without doubtful disputations." All are told to grow into the knowledge of Christ, and if "in anything ye are otherwise minded God will reveal even this unto you."

Such being the case, differences are to be expected among

the children of God. Not being perfectly sanctified, they will see some things differently and will act differently therefore. In other words, the theology of the Bible is the theology of denominations. One person will think that God forbids him to use the organ in his public worship; another will not. They must unfortunately divide. One will think he should sing only Psalms; others do not agree. They must unfortunately divide. One will think that the government of the Church should be episcopal; another, presbyterian; another, congregational. Unfortunately they must divide. Furthermore, many of the divisions are rather natural ones along natural cultural and historical lines which do not indicate any real division in spirit.

But is this as disastrous for those outside as it might at first appear? We think not. It will be confusing we cannot doubt, but not hopelessly confusing. And there are some things which will become all the more clearly apparent. For one thing, it will be clear that these different groups have not given up their intellectual integrity and autonomy. The only way to prevent differences is to prevent thinking. As long as there is freedom of thought among men in their present state, they will not be without differences. The differences may be confusing, to be sure, but just as surely they bear eloquent testimony to vigor and integrity of thought. Uniformity may not be so confusing, but it may bear testimony to slavishness and extreme docility.

Another advantage which emerges from the divided state of the churches may be surprising, namely, the revelation of their unity. Indeed, theirs is a division which accentuates unity, for it points to something more than division. They remain Christian denominations, or rather, divisions within Christianity. There is something held in common by the differing groups, a common loyalty to the Christian faith. In spite of all the variations among the denominations, there is an area of basic agreement which leads them all to claim the name of Christian and to be acknowledged by one another as Christian. They all hold to a "common denominational" of belief. Differ as they may, they do not differ at the center of things. They all acknowledge Jesus Christ as God and Saviour and trust in Him alone and seek to be obedient to Him. They differ in their understanding of what He commands, but they agree in their intention to be obedient to His will.

Combining the two ideas we see freedom under law. The freedom is manifest in the variety of the expressions of Christian faith. The law is seen in the common desire to know and do the will of Christ. This is a testimony which denominations, by virtue of their being denominations, give; and this is a testimony which, in this world of sin and error, only denominations can give. And inasmuch as it is extremely important that they should bear witness to this great truth, it is good that denominations exist, as long as the differences exist.

We will not deny that there is sometimes unhappy rivalry among Christian denominations that ill befits those who profess to regard one another as brethren redeemed by a common Saviour. But a positive word can be said even at this point. Sometimes Christians oppose one another for conscience' sake. Without calling in question another's sincerity, there may be a question of his wisdom or understanding. One group, feeling that Christ would have them do things so and so, may think that another group errs grievously in the matter and must be opposed even to the point of unsightly competition. This may be unfortunate, but one may still admire the zeal and integrity behind the action, and feel less indignant when he sees things as others see them.

Furthermore, it must be remembered that this unchristian type of rivalry among Christian groups is not really so common as it is sometimes represented. Most churches freely commune with one another, join together in common enterprises for the total welfare of the community, associate with one another in unions of churches, make common testimonies to the world, and engage in common charities for the world. All in all, there is far more co-operation among churches than unwholesome rivalry.

The third and last charge against Christians which we will consider is that they are so often "holier-than-thou's." They feel and act as if they were superior to other people. They draw their skirts about them and keep at a distance from others for fear of contamination. They enjoy making other people miserable and are naturally inclined to throw a wet blanket on anything which has any pleasure in it. "Thou shalt not" is their motto, and being around them is distinctly depressing.

Now it will be apparent to anyone that all of these criticisms—which are usually given in the same context—are hardly consistent. It is difficult for any person to be aloof and a kill-joy at the same time. To be a kill-joy a person simply has to be a mixer of sorts. And at the point of his being a kill-joy he obviously is not aloof enough. Be that as it may, this type of criticism is far from uncommon; and because Christian people are thought to be of this character, others are sometimes reluctant to be associated with them.

Again we must admit that there is some truth here. Some Christian people are sanctimonious and exude an odor of false piety. They feel themselves to be above and superior to other persons. They seem to think that they are good and deserve the honor of God and the envy of men. At the time of Jesus, the leading religious people were of this sort, and Christ had constantly to be warning His disciples of the "leaven of the Pharisees." He told these self-righteous ones that harlots and publicans would enter the Kingdom before them.

In the rebuke of Jesus lies the first part of the answer to this criticism. Not only does the world disapprove of the censorious and sanctimonious, but Christ and true religion also disapprove of them. They ought not to be members of the Church, and it is worse for them that they are. They are the real hypocrites, and their condemnation will be all the greater for their much pretending. In other words, the message of the Church, instead of encouraging such a disposition, is utterly opposed to it. Hypocrites come into the Church and remain there under false pretenses.

The second answer is a continuation of the first. Christianity, so far from producing this type of person, has every tendency to overcome the spirit of hypocrisy in its adherents. Every person has some arrogance and vanity about him, and the message of Christianity, by preaching humility in the words, and supremely in the example, of Jesus, tends to drive out this evil spirit. If a man is proud it is in spite of his Christianity, and if he is humble it is because of it.

In the third place, people often make the charge of "holier than thou" falsely. Sometimes they call by that name anyone who refuses to do what he thinks is wrong. This is manifestly unfair. If any man regards a particular practice as evil, he is morally obliged to refrain from it although the rest of the world may engage in it. He may not thereby regard himself as holier than the rest of the world. He may well believe that what he thinks is wrong someone else may practice in good conscience and even be more truly moral in the wrong act than he himself is in the right one. He knows that it takes far more than one act to constitute a moral person. Furthermore, he may be very conscious of his own shortcomings in many other ways. And he may believe that his abstention from one particular practice which he thinks is wrong is owing only to the grace of God. He may regard it as an act of grace that he recognizes the nature of the act when others do not. So that even in that particular point he may be humble rather than proud.

In the fourth place, even positive criticism of an act, beyond merely abstaining from it, is not proof of a "holier-than-thou" disposition. A person may recognize the moral or immoral character of a particular practice better than another and say so without thinking that he is therefore more holy, but merely more understanding. He may well know that the devil is able to criticize far better than he. But a well-developed critical faculty does not prove the devil's love for truth and goodness, nor that he is holier than men. The Christian may be constrained to speak against the practice, not because he is the enemy of society, but the friend of it. He does not want to kill the joy of his friends, but to keep them from an apparent joy that really will, in a sense, kill them. If he hated society, he would let it go on to hurt itself; but because he loves it, he must seek to prevent its hurting itself. Because he recognizes the subtlety of sin and its mischievous results in his life and experience, he must warn others against it. In so doing, he may be quite the opposite of "holier-than-thou" in attitude.

In the fifth place, he must hold himself aloof from those who insist on doing what he thinks is wrong. This is not because he hates men, but because he loves them. This is not because he wants to separate from them, but because he wants them, for their own good, to be separate from sin. He is anxious to be with men rather than apart from them. But he must be with them to do them good not harm. And to be with them in their evil is to do them harm and not good. He will gladly be with them in innocent things. He desires to be their friend. And he wants them to know of his Lord that He may become their Lord. In that sense, he, as his Lord before him, is the "friend of publicans and sinners" while, as his Lord before him, he does not keep company with them who are engaged in evil practices.

Summing the matter up, let us say that the Church confesses the presence of "holier-than-thou's" in her communion. She asks those outside who are justly offended by these persons to remember that she does not encourage them, that she warns against their attitude, and that the entire tendency of her teaching is to overcome this spirit in them. Furthermore, she would ask a critical world to look more closely at some of those whom they criticize to see if indeed in every case they are guilty of being "holier-than-thou." She suggests that if they will so examine the matter, they will see the behavior of some to be far more commendable than censurable, to be, indeed, the very course of action which they who feel the sting of its reproof need most to see and by which they are most likely to be profited.

PART V

CONCLUSION

25

The Pragmatic Test

WE HAVE taken a long journey. It began with our noticing that many are presently concerned with faith. We wondered about ourselves. Consequently, we faced at the outset some difficulties which often confront persons and dissuade them from a more thorough investigation of Christianity. These questions considered and obviated, we began our investigation.

The first step in our investigation was to investigate the investigator. We tried to show that our minds are reliable guides to truth, or else there is no meaning to be found anywhere by any means. Equipped then with a reliance on a careful and critical use of our reason, we began to consider the arguments for the existence and nature of a divine being.

Reflection on the nature of men and things led us to belief in the being of an eternal, intelligent, self-caused, moral Being we called God. But we realized that much was still lacking. There were many other questions which needed answering to which nature held no key. It was apparent to us that none but this divine Being, of whose existence we had learned, could possibly disclose the knowledge we still so much needed. It seemed to us likely that He would do so. In other words, we came to the conviction that there was a need for special revelation and a likelihood that it could be found. Thus we came to consider the Bible and its claims to inspiration. We found internal evidence and also external evidence (from the authority of Christ) that this Bible is indeed the needed and expected Word of God. Archaeological studies, we noted, tend to confirm this view of the reliability of Scripture.

So we examined the main teaching of the Bible in order to have a systematic understanding of its message. As difficulties emerged, we considered some of its doctrines particularly and the criticisms which are sometimes urged against them. Then we compared the message of Christianity with the teachings of the other religions of the world, seeing by the comparison the manifest superiority of the religion of the Bible.

The fact that the Bible answered the questions posed by nature and that it alone answered them made it presumptive that the Bible was indeed the Word of God. But we found further evidence for its authority when we considered the miracles of the Bible and especially those attributed to Jesus Christ. Likewise, the argument from the fulfillment of predictive prophecy further tended to buttress the case for the Bible and Christianity.

The ultimate proof of the divinity of the Christian religion was its influence in the world during the past twenty centuries. This influence we considered in the affairs of history and institutions. And more particularly, we examined the influence of Christ on individuals such as martyrs.

Before concluding our journey we turned aside to face certain objections intended to dissuade us from faith. We considered arguments drawn from certain types of evolutionary theory. We considered the charge that all things are determined and that truth is only what a person has been taught to think that it is. We noticed some of the criticisms which have been urged against the reliability of the Bible. And we concluded with a consideration of the criticisms which are made against Christians themselves and presented as arguments against the truth of Christianity. To all of these arguments we have tried to give honest and respectful attention. We have treated the objectors as honest and respectful persons. We have assumed that their objections have proceeded from sincere doubts, and we have attempted humbly to present evidence which speaks accurately and adequately to the points which they raised. We trust that we have made out some "reasons for faith."

If this were a text in mathematics rather than religion, the discussion of the principles would be followed by the assignment of some problems which test and confirm these principles. Or in a science course there would be some laboratory experiments made. Such assignments are not likely to be made in a course in Christian evidences, although perhaps they could be.

But whether such laboratory work is required in a given course or not, it is required in the life of every person who would know in experience the truth of these things. All these things have been written that you might believe. But if you believe, you must practice. Faith has an intellectual element to be sure. Although that element is what has mainly concerned us in a book, there are other aspects which concern us in life. Faith, in addition to its intellectual element, has also emotional and volitional elements. That is, for a true act of belief there must be understanding, feeling, and will, synthesized in the individual person. Having grasped the argument and been persuaded by it, we should feel drawn to it and should resolutely decide to live by it. If the argument is really persuasive and we do not feel joy in submitting our lives to the religion which it argues, then we stand condemned by our own understanding. We are hearers of the Word but not doers. We know but do not practice. He that hath much light and doeth not the master's will, he shall be beaten with many stripes, Christ says. So testing all these things in the crucible of one's own soul is essential in religion as truly as in any science.

Indeed, laboratory work is more essential in religion than in science. You can understand truths in mathematics and science without working them out. Working them out does not give new understanding but really only fixes the principles in the understanding and in the memory. But the beauty (in distinction from the truth) of religion can be known only by coming to Christ, resting in Him, obeying Him, having faith in Him. Art really offers a truer analogy to the religious situation than science. Aesthetic beauty can be described and conceived, but there is still a great difference between the beautiful as described and the beautiful as seen. There is something in the seeing that cannot be conveyed by the description however exact it may be.

Christ has said that if any man will do God's will, "he shall know of the doctrine, whether it be of God, or whether I speak of myself." Here is allusion to a dimension of knowledge not limited to the intellectual. It clearly refers to the experiential. For it is apparent that any person with reasonable mind can "know" that Christ spoke from God quite apart from any doing of His will. There are conclusive arguments to prove that Christ is the Son of God, whether one ever agrees to do Christ's will or not. Indeed we think that the argument of this book may be as well understood by non-Christians as by Christians. But the non-Christian can only understand it as an argument and nothing more than that. On the other hand, the person who understands the argument and submits himself to Christ's will shall gain a knowledge which can come no other way. Thus a highly intelligent unbeliever could well master this book so as to state the argument better than many a less gifted believer. But the believer, however few his gifts, will have more of this experiential knowledge than the most gifted unbeliever. Indeed it is not a matter of more and less, but of some and none. The least gifted believer will have some of this knowledge, and the most gifted unbeliever will have none whatever.

This is the laboratory part of Christianity, whether it be part of a course in the Christian religion or not. It may be the end of a course of reading, but it is only the beginning of Christian experience. A person may get an "A" in a course and flunk in Christianity. This book is an argument for Christianity. The reader may grasp the argument without accepting the Christianity to which the argument points. Thus he may gain his credit for a course and lose eternal life.

The book leaves you at this point. You are on your own. From here on you are alone with Christ. The book can bring you to consider Him and give you some reasons for faith in Him, but it cannot believe for you. It can reason for you, but it can not exercise faith for you. It can bring you to faith, but you alone can do the believing.

It is the prayer of the author for his readers that you may believe and that believing you may obey and that obeying you may "know."

Bibliography

ALEXANDER, ARCHIBALD. *Evidences of the Authenticity, Inspiration, and Canonical Authority of the Holy Scriptures.* Philadelphia: Presbyterian Board of Publication, 1836.

ANDREWS, ELIAS. *Modern Humanism and Christian Theism.* With a Foreword by Rev. James S. Thomson. Grand Rapids: Zondervan Publishing House, 1939.

AQUINAS, THOMAS. *On the Truth of the Catholic Faith. Summa Contra Gentiles.* Translated, with an Introduction and Notes by Anton C. Pegis. Garden City, N. Y.: Image Books, 1955.

BAILLIE, JOHN. *Invitation to Pilgrimage.* New York: Charles Scribner's Sons, 1942.

BARNES, ALBERT. *The Evidences of Christianity in the Nineteenth Century. Being the First Course of Lectures on the "Ely Foundation" of the Union Theological Seminary.* New York, London, Glasgow: Blackie and Son, 1871.

BEARDSLEY, FRANK GRENVILLE. *The Christ of the Ages.* New York: American Tract Society, 1941.

BEATTIE, FRANCIS ROBERT. *Apologetics; or, The Rational Vindication of Christianity, with an Introduction by Benjamin B. Warfield.* Richmond: Presbyterian Committee of Publications, 1903.

BELL, BERNARD IDDINGS. *Beyond Agnosticism. A Book for Tired Mechanists.* New York: Harper & Brothers, 1929.

BERKELEY, GEORGE, Bp. of Cloyne. *Alciphron; or The Minute Philosopher.* In Seven Dialogues containing an Apology for the Christian Religion, Against Those Who are Called Free-thinkers. The First American Edition from the Fourth London Edition. New York: from Sydney's Press for Increase Cooke and Co., 1803.

BERKOUWER, GERRIT CORNELIS. *Modern Uncertainty and Christian Faith.* Grand Rapids: W. B. Eerdmans Publishing Co., 1953.

Bridgewater Treatises on the Power, Wisdom, and Goodness of God as Manifested in the Creation. London: William Pickering, 1834.

BRUCE, ALEXANDER BALMAIN. *Apologetics; or, Christianity Defensively Stated.* 12th ed. New York: Charles Scribner's Sons, 1912.

BUTTRICK, GEORGE ARTHUR. *The Christian Fact and Modern Doubt; A Preface* to a Restatement of Christian Faith. New York: Charles Scribner's Sons, 1934.

CAILLIET, ÉMILE. *The Beginning of Wisdom.* Westwood, N. J.: Fleming H. Revell Co., 1947.

CAIRNS, DAVID. *The Reasonableness of the Christian Faith.* London, New York, etc.: Hodder & Stoughton, 1909.

CAIRNS, JOHN. *Christ the Principal Evidence of Christianity.* Westwood, N. J.: Fleming H. Revell, 1893.

CANDLISH, ROBERT SMITH. *Reason and Revelation.* London: Thomas Nelson & Sons, 1859.

CARNELL, EDWARD JOHN. *An Introduction to Christian Apologetics, A Philosophic Defense of the Trinitarian-Theistic Faith.* Grand Rapids: W. B. Eerdmans Publishing Co., 1948.

————. *Christian Commitment, An Apologetic.* New York: The Macmillan Company, 1957.

CARPENTER, WILLIAM BOYD, Bp. of Ripon. *The Witness to the Influence of Christ; being the William Delten Noble Lectures for 1904, by the Rt. Rev. William Boyd Carpenter, D.T., Bishop of Ripon.* Boston and New York: Odin, Methelin and Company, 1905.

CHALMERS, THOMAS. *The Evidence and the Authority of the Christian Revelation.* 6th ed. Andover: Mark Gilman, 1818.

————. *On the Miraculous and Internal Evidences of the Christian Revelation, and the Authority of Its Records.* 2 vols. New York: Carter & Brothers, 1854.

CHATEAUBRIAND, FRANÇOIS AUGSTE RENÉ. *The Genius of Christianity; or, The Spirit and Beauty of the Christian Religion. A new not complete translation from the French, with a Preface, Biographical Notice of the Author, and Typical and Explanatory Notes, by Charles I. White.* 2nd rev. ed. Baltimore: John Murphy & Co.; London: Charles Dolman, 1856.

CLARK, GORDON HADDON. *A Christian View of Men and Things.* Grand Rapids: W. B. Eerdmans Publishing Co., 1952.

CUNNINGHAM, WILLIAM. *Theological Lectures on Subjects Connected with Natural Theology, Evidences of Christianity, the Canon and Inspiration of Scripture.* New York: Carter, 1878.

DEVRIES, JOHN. *Beyond the Atom; An Appraisal of Our Christian Faith in this Age of Atomic Science.* Grand Rapids: W. B. Eerdmans Publishing Co., 1948.

DORCHESTER, DANIEL. *Christianity Vindicated by Its Enemies.* New York: Hunt & Co., Inc.; Cincinnati: Granston & Curts, 1896.

EBRARD, JOHANN HEINRICH AUGUST. *Apologetics, or, A Scientific Vindication of Christianity translated by William Stuart . . . and . . . John Macpherson,* 3 vols. Edinburgh: T. & T. Clark, 1886-1887.

FARRAR, FREDERIC WILLIAM. *Witness of History to Christ. Five Sermons Preached Before the University of Cambridge; Being the Hulsean Lectures for the Year 1870.* London, New York: Macmillan & Co., 1906.

FISHER, GEORGE MARK. *The Grounds of Theistic and Christian Belief.* London: Hodder and Stoughton, 1892.

————. *Manual of Christian Evidences.* New York: Charles Scribner's Sons, 1888.

GARVIE, ALFRED ERNEST. *A Handbook of Christian Apologetics.* New York: Charles Scribner's Sons, 1913.

GILSON, ÉTIENNE. *Christianity and Philosophy*, translated by Ralph MacDonald, c.s.p. New York, London: Pub. for the Institute of Mediaeval Studies by Sheed & Ward, 1939.

GODET, FREDERIC. *Lectures in Defence of the Christian Faith*, translated by W. H. Lyttelton. 4th ed. Edinburgh: T. & T. Clark, after 1883.

HARKNESS, GEORGIA ELMA. *The Modern Rival of Christian Faith; An Analysis of Secularism*. Nashville: Abingdon Press, 1952.

HENRY, CARL FERDINAND HOWARD. *Remaking the Modern Mind*. 2nd ed. Grand Rapids: W. B. Eerdmans Publishing Company, 1948.

————. *Giving a Reason for Our Hope*. Boston: W. A. Wilde Co., 1949.

HICKS, LEWIS EZRA. *A Critique of Design-Arguments; A Historical Review and Re-examination of the Methods of Reasoning in Natural Theology*. New York: Charles Scribner's Sons, 1883.

HODGSON, LEONARD. *The Place of Reason in Christian Apologetics; Four Lectures Delivered Before the General Theological Seminary, New York*. Oxford: B. Blackwell, 1925.

HOPKINS, MARK. *Evidences of Christianity*. Lectures before the Lowell Institute, revised as a text-book, with a supplementary chapter considering some attacks on the critical school, the corroborative evidence of recently discovered manuscripts, etc., and testimony of Jesus on his trial. Presentation ed. on the Bross Foundation, Lake Forest College. Boston: T. R. Marvin & Son, 1909.

HORDERN, WILLIAM EDWARD. *Christianity, Communism, and History*. Nashville: Abingdon Press, 1954.

JEFFERSON, CHARLES EDWARD. *Things Fundamental; A Course of Thirteen Discourses in Modern Apologetics*. New York: Thomas Y. Crowell & Company, 1903.

JOHNSON, WILLIAM HALLOCK. *The Christian Faith under Modern Searchlights*. Westwood, N. J.: Fleming H. Revell Company, 1916. (The L. P. Stone lectures delivered at Princeton Theological Seminary.)

KEITH, ALEXANDER. *Evidence of the Truth of the Christian Religion, Derived from the Literal Fulfillment of Prophecy; Particularly as Illustrated by the History of the Jews, and by the Discoveries of Recent Travellers*. Philadelphia: Presbyterian Board of Publication, 1844.

KELLOGG, SAMUEL HENRY. *A Handbook of Comparative Religion*. Philadelphia: The Westminster Press, 1899.

KEYSER, LEANDER SYLVESTER. *A System of Christian Evidence*. 4th rev. ed. Burlington, Iowa: Lutheran Literary Board, 1926.

LEWIS, CLYDE STAPLES. *The Case for Christianity*, published in England under the title "Broadcast Talks." New York: The Macmillan Company, 1943.

LOCKE, JOHN. *The Reasonableness of Christianity, as Delivered in the Scriptures. To which are added, An Essay on the Understanding of St. Paul's Epistles; and a Discourse on Miracles*. With a biographical essay, and appendix, and notes, by a layman. London: George Virtue, 1850.

MACARTNEY, CLARENCE EDWARD NOBLE. *Christian Faith and the Spirit of the Age*. New York: American Tract Society, 1940.

MACDONALD, RICHARDSON ALLEN. *Christian Apologetics*. New York: Harper & Brothers, 1927.

MACGREGOR, JAMES. *Studies in the History of Christian Apologetics, New Testament and Post-Apostolic.* Edinburgh: T. & T. Clark, 1894.

McCOSH, JAMES. *Biblical Forms and Special Ends in Creation, by Rev. James McCosh . . . and George Dickie.* New York: Harper & Brothers, 1856.

MICKLEM, NATHANIEL. *Ultimate Questions.* Nashville: Abingdon Presss, 1955.

MULLINS, EDGAR YOUNG. *Why Is Christianity True? Christian Evidences.* Thin edition. Philadelphia: American Baptist Publication Society, 1911.

ORR, JAMES. *The Faith of a Modern Christian.* New York: Hodder and Stoughton, 1910.

——. *The Christian View of God and the World as Centring in the Incarnation, Being the First Series of Kerr Lectures.* 3rd ed. New York: Charles Scribner's Sons, 1897.

PIERSON, ARTHUR TAPPAN. *The Gordian Knot; or, The Problem Which Baffles Infidelity.* New York and London: Funk & Wagnalls Company, 1902.

——. *"Many Infallible Proofs": The Evidences of Christianity.* Westwood, N. J.: Fleming H. Revell, 1886.

RAMM, BERNARD. *The Christian View of Science and Scripture.* 1st ed. Grand Rapids: W. B. Eerdmans Publishing Co., 1954.

——. *Protestant Christian Evidences.* Chicago: Moody Press, 1953.

RICHARDSON, ALAN. *Christian Apologetics.* New York: Harper & Brothers, 1948.

ROGERS, CLEMENT FRANCIS. *The Case for Christianity, An Outline of Popular Apologetics.* New York: Harper & Brothers, 1928.

Index